Preparing for Educational Administration Using Case Analysis

Karen L. Hanson
National University

Merrill
Prentice Hall

Upper Saddle River, New Jersey
Columbus, Ohio

Library of Congress Cataloging-in-Publication Data
Hanson, Karen L.
    Preparing for educational administration using case analysis / by Karen L. Hanson.
      p. cm.
    Includes index.
    ISBN 0-13-023024-3
      1. School administrators—Training of—United States. 2. School management and
organization—United States—Case studies. 3. School administrators—United States—Case
studies. I. Title.

LB1738.5 .H35 2001
371.2'00973—dc21   99-086443

Vice President and Publisher: Jeffery W. Johnston
Executive Editor: Debra A. Stollenwerk
Editor: Linda Scharp McElhiney
Editorial Assistant: Penny S. Burleson
Production Editor: Linda Hillis Bayma
Design Coordinator: Diane C. Lorenzo
Cover Designer: Dean Barrett
Cover art: © PhotoDisc
Production Manager: Pamela D. Bennett
Production Coordination and Text Design: Carlisle Publishers Services
Director of Marketing: Kevin Flanagan
Marketing Manager: Amy June
Marketing Services Manager: Krista Groshong

This book was set in Korinna by Carlisle Communications, Ltd. It was printed and bound by Courier Kendallville, Inc. The cover was printed by Courier Kendallville, Inc.

10 9 8 7 6 5 4 3 2 1
ISBN 0-13-023024-3

To my grandchildren, who remind me every day that the human experience can be enriched by the stories we tell, the problems we solve, and the lessons we learn.

Preface

This book was written for individuals who are interested in pursuing a career in educational administration. It offers a unique opportunity to engage in case analysis, meaningful discussion, lively debate, and serious problem solving with case material that is relevant and realistic and that captures the interest of the reader. The primary purpose of the book is to introduce cases that represent real-life situations in today's schools and to provide a case analysis framework as a tool for analyzing the cases and resolving the problem(s) presented in each case.

The book is a valuable resource for university professors, educational administration students, school districts, county offices of education, group seminar leaders, and specific workshop trainers who believe, as I do, that theory without practice is a waste of time for individuals who aspire to become educational administrators.

The 34 cases presented in the text provide practical experiences in case analysis for individuals who are preparing for educational administration, and they motivate students to pursue research for additional information to adequately address the problems identified in the cases. The cases represent diverse and culturally rich examples of some of the issues school administrators experience. Included are traditional subjects such as curriculum and instruction, leadership, employee and community relations, budget and finance, governance and law, student conduct, technology, and special education. Also included are more sensitive subjects such as race and gender relations, health and welfare, conflict management, ethics, and diversity.

The matrix on page 3 lists specific topics and corresponding case subject matter. A suggested reading list is provided at the end of the cases that includes references for research and information useful for the case analysis process.

Each case has four specific sections. The first section focuses on the people, place, and culture of the school community and provides background for the case. The second section introduces a problem or problems that need to be resolved, and the third section offers questions that are intended to guide the student through the problem-solving process. The questions also serve to prompt students to consider additional strategies for resolving the various problems that are presented. The fourth and final section lists one or more activities that are designed to help students further develop their problem-solving skills and practice what they have learned as a result of the case analysis process.

The case analysis framework in the Introduction provides a tool for systematically processing the information in the cases, categorizing the data, summarizing the material, and locating the source of the primary case problem so the problem-solving process can begin. The framework helps isolate the problem and helps readers respond effectively to the questions at the end of each case. At the conclusion of each case, there is a page provided for the reader's own notes about the case.

An example of how to use and apply the case analysis framework appears after the first case, "Is There a Nurse in the House?"

Although the book is intended to be fiction and all the names are fictitious, many of the cases present very real possibilities, and some of them portray events similar to those experienced by educational leaders in schools across the United States.

As you read the cases and use the case analysis framework, you will develop a unique foundation of skills for addressing the challenges that school leaders experience. This book is a must-read for students of educational leadership who wish to take on this challenge to provide a quality educational environment for children.

ACKNOWLEDGMENTS

I wish to thank the following individuals who contributed substantially to the development, content, and story lines for several of the cases in this book: Gary Hoban, Lynne Anderson, John Carta-Falsa, Mark Miller, Bernard Balanay, Roberta Rose, Julie Burke, Maria Castilleja, Timothy Glover, Deborah Huggins, R. Y. Jackson, Gloria McKearney, Suzanne Miyasaki, Staci Monreal, C. Pebley, Linda Rees, Mel Schuler, Tom Spence, Margaret Steinrichter, Nancy Intermill, Rae Correira, Deborah Costanzo, Shelley Peterson, Linda Choy, Karen Mooney, Kyle Ruggles, Julie Burke, F. Steve Kennedy, Jr., Shelley Petersen, Katie Langford, Cheryl Bowen, Laurie Francis, Deborah Costanzo, and Rae Correira.

I also wish to express my deepest appreciation to my husband, Gregory, who stood by me when I was tired and offered endless hours of editing—not to mention a good cup of coffee when I needed it.

The reviewers of this book provided valuable insight: Reene Alley, Youngstown State University; Dale Brubaker, University of North Carolina–Greensboro; Carol Carter-Lowery, Central Connecticut State University; Larry W. Hughes, University of Houston; and Price M. Michael, State University of West Georgia. I would also like to express my gratitude to Linda Scharp McElhiney, Acquisitions Editor, who became my friend and colleague. I appreciate her support throughout this project. Finally, I wish to extend my appreciation to Executive Editor Debbie Stollenwerk, who continued to keep me informed and reminded me that deadlines are a good thing.

Contents

Introduction

THE CONTEXT

The primary responsibility of school leaders is to oversee the operation of educational institutions to ensure that teachers teach and students learn. The challenges that administrators face can be overwhelming because of an influential and politically motivated environment that demands more than simply an allegiance to teaching and learning. School administrators need to learn how to balance theory with practice, the ideal with reality, and to establish a middle ground on which to operate.

A career in school administration is particularly difficult at the present time because of a multitude of influences affecting students and teachers. Classroom teachers, students, and school leaders are intensely scrutinized by individuals from all walks of life who claim to have the remedy for what ails education. Partnerships between public and private schools, collaborations between industry and education, and a controversial union of state and religious interests are some examples of influences that affect the way schools operate.

The situation is further complicated because the infrastructure that supports education in America is fragmented and lacks the structural continuity needed to facilitate the transformation that is taking place. As an example, the decision makers in the United States have not agreed on whether national performance standards for students should be applied at the state level or how state-mandated standards should work with federal standards. Additionally, some states use both state-mandated curriculum frameworks and textbooks, whereas other states allow local schools to create their own curricula and expect teachers to choose the textbooks students use.

There is an ongoing controversy surrounding student performance. How should teachers assess students? What tests should be administered? How should test scores be interpreted to measure academic competency? Furthermore, the discussion concerning norm-referenced versus criterion-referenced tests and which tests are preferred to measure performance outcomes is far from being resolved. Additionally, the issue of grade level exam requirements is unresolved as is the coordination of local, state, and federal examinations to reflect consistent assessment.

The United States lacks a uniform policy that addresses the collection and distribution of revenue to support its educational system. Inequity exists between states and also between districts within some states in terms of the money spent per child to educate students in schools.

Program initiatives such as parental choice and the voucher system create an imbalance in the education status quo. Legislators and business interests complicate the ongoing deliberation by competing for political and financial profit, such as promoting the use of public funds for private school placement including religious schools. Additionally, representatives from special interest groups have gained support in recent years by running for school board positions and by supporting elected officials who sympathize with their causes.

Adding to this unstable condition are teacher training programs that reflect major inconsistencies. For example, in some states, a fifth year in an institution of higher education is mandated by accreditation agencies for teacher certification, whereas other states have no such requirement. Furthermore, a few states require additional tests in subject matter curriculum, whereas other states do not have the same requirement for certification.

Future teachers are discouraged by these discrepancies in the system, and the United States is slow in responding to the challenges that many states face as the demand for new teachers increases because of early teacher retirement, a high rate of teacher turnover, and insufficient salaries to recruit the best and brightest candidates for the teaching profession. Additionally, methods for evaluating teacher performance vary considerably.

Today's schools need strong leadership and well-prepared and educated administrators who understand the complexity of the educational system, can solve problems, and have the commitment to raise the benchmark for educational programs and performance in America's schools.

We need caring professionals who are willing and able to take on the challenges that school leadership brings. Individuals who sign up for the job of educational administrators face an exciting time. They will be challenged to advance creative ideas, preserve successful policies and programs, and solve problems that otherwise would prevent them from accomplishing their goals.

THE CASES

In order to prepare for their futures, teachers whose goal is to become educational administrators will benefit from analyzing cases that represent different types of problems occurring in schools. The matrix illustrated in Figure 1 outlines specific topics of concern to educational administrators and identifies the cases that particularly address those issues. The cases are intended to stimulate classroom discussion, encourage problem solving, and promote an interest in the research needed to advance an understanding of the content and problems introduced.

THE PURPOSE

It is worthwhile to remember that the value of analyzing cases is to enhance the practical side of preparing for educational administration while relying on meaningful research to strengthen the problem-solving experience. Combining theory and practice offers a realistic balance to the educational administration process, and it fosters a dedication to understanding the research as it applies to everyday life. School administrators are individuals who welcome these challenges, commit to the charge, and believe that children are worth it.

Analyzing case studies to prepare for a career as an educational administrator can be a useful exercise in the art of problem solving. Attend to the cases. If you simply read the cases and answer the questions, you may not develop the insight and appreciation of knowledge or gain in internalizing the case study to improve your problem-solving skills. The cases should be treated as real situations, and the analysis should be undertaken with the intention of actually making decisions and resolving the problems at issue.

FIGURE 1 Matrix

Cases

Topics	1	2	3	4	5	6	7	8	9	10	11	12	13	14	15	16	17	18	19	20	21	22	23	24	25	26	27	28	29	30	31	32	33	34
Curriculum/ Instruction		X	X			X		X						X		X	X	X	X		X	X	X			X		X				X		
Leadership						X		X			X			X		X	X	X	X		X	X	X	X		X		X		X		X		
Employee Relations		X	X						X				X					X	X					X	X						X			
Race and Gender Relations					X	X						X			X		X						X							X				
Student Conduct			X	X	X		X					X			X											X							X	
Health and Welfare	X						X				X	X		X						X						X	X		X		X		X	X
Community Relations	X				X	X			X	X	X			X			X	X		X		X		X		X	X	X				X		X
Budget and Finance				X				X						X		X		X			X		X						X			X		X
Conflict Management			X					X		X		X	X					X				X			X			X						X
Ethics		X			X				X					X	X	X			X										X					X
Governance and Politics	X	X		X	X	X			X	X	X			X	X	X	X	X	X			X	X	X		X	X	X		X		X		
Special Education	X	X				X	X	X				X										X			X									
Diversity	X	X	X			X	X								X		X	X			X	X	X			X			X	X				
Technology		X									X										X	X		X										

HANSON'S CASE ANALYSIS FRAMEWORK

I have designed a case analysis framework (see Figure 2) to assist you in analyzing the cases. The process of analyzing the cases is detailed in the following steps:

1. Summarize the case.
2. Identify the problem in a single sentence.
3. Select specific information from the case and categorize it according to people, place, or program.
4. Review and prioritize the information.
5. Refer to the data in each category to solve the problem identified in the case and to respond to the case study questions.

An example of how to use the case analysis framework is provided at the end of Case 1, "Is There a Nurse in the House?"

Each case offers a different background with a unique problem to solve. Depending on the specifics of the case, it is possible that the most significant data are concentrated in one of the three categories (people, place, program) or contained in a combination of two or more categories, depending on the case.

As a final note, you are encouraged to conduct appropriate research and investigate district, state, and federal mandates that relate to each case to develop a responsible foundation for analyzing the cases and solving the problems presented.

As future educational leaders, it is up to you to meet the challenge.

FIGURE 2 *Hanson's Case Analysis Framework*

Case 1

Is There a Nurse in the House?

The population of Summerset is growing at a rapid pace, and new housing developments are continuously being built for moderate- to high-income families. The community has become a close partner with the school district and participates in the district's annual summit meetings where specific goals and objectives are established. Community members actively support individual schools by promoting funding initiatives and volunteering to work in the schools.

Challenger School District is located in the heart of Summerset and serves approximately 50,000 students. Although 70 percent of the school district's population is Hispanic, Discovery High School, which is the only high school in the district, reflects a more ethnically balanced population. The school provides educational services for a population of 35 percent Hispanic, 30 percent Caucasian, 20 percent Pacific Islanders, and 20 percent African American students.

With an enrollment of 1,900 students, Discovery High provides a variety of programs to students in grades 9 through 12. Additionally, it provides support for students with special needs particularly for the gifted and talented students, for those with limited English proficiency, and for students with other special education needs.

The high school staff includes 120 teachers, 3 assistant principals, 5 counselors, 2 part-time campus security staff, an itinerant psychologist, and the usual classified support personnel. The school is highly thought of in the community because of the faculty's commitment toward interdisciplinary teaching. Additionally, students have the opportunity to focus their studies in specific areas of interest such as fine arts, multimedia, technology, and engineering.

School activities and events are widely featured in two of the most popularly read newspapers and are highlighted on the local television station. School board members visit the site frequently and at least three of them are currently running for city council. The school board members are divided on numerous issues including personnel, school operations, race relations, and program funding.

The superintendent is serving his second year, prior to which, he was employed as the assistant superintendent in the same school district.

Special interest groups have had a strong influence on the election of school board members and the selection of superintendents. Included in the list of influential groups are the Latino Coalition, the Special Education Parent Advocate Group, and the 504 Disability Act Committee.

For this case, assume that you are one of the assistant principals at Discovery High School.

THE PROBLEM

The school principal and two of your colleagues, who are also assistant principals, are attending a state conference off site for four days. The principal has charged you with managing the school and has specifically requested that you address a problem with one of the parents, Mrs. Carlton.

Two of her sons, John and Abraham, are enrolled at the high school, and they both have cerebral palsy. They have attended Discovery High for the past two years. Each one of Mrs. Carlton's sons is an excellent student, and they are both enrolled in honors classes and have been mainstreamed into regular education classes for the entire school day. A registered nurse is assigned to each of the boys. During school hours, the nurses are available to tend to the boys' needs and are compensated by the school district.

Mrs. Carlton has issued several verbal complaints to the principal and the special education program director regarding John's nurse, Mrs. Adams. According to Mrs. Carlton, Mrs. Adams is often late meeting John's bus in the morning, and so the bus leaves for John's school without Mrs. Adams. Mrs. Carlton is concerned because, even though her other son's nurse is on the school bus, there have been times when both boys needed medical attention simultaneously. In the past, some situations have been so severe that Mrs. Carlton has described them as medical emergencies.

A few months ago, Mrs. Carlton issued a written complaint requesting the dismissal of Mrs. Adams. The principal met with John's parents and Mrs. Adams to discuss the situation, and an agreement was reached to assign Mrs. Adams to another school in the district. In the meantime, Mrs. Carlton decided to keep John at home until the school district found a new nurse for him. The district informed Mrs. Carlton that it would take at least eight weeks to hire a new nurse.

In the principal's absence, you decide to address Mrs. Carlton's concerns by locating a teacher in the school who is willing to work at John's home with him. In addition, you suggest to the special education program director that she contact a temporary employment agency in town who you believe has nurses available for immediate placement.

The director of special education contacts your office to inform you that the agency has a nurse available for employment. She also informs you that the school district's director of human resources has agreed to hire the nurse from the agency.

You decide to contact Mrs. Carlton immediately and share with her the good news. She is delighted that John will be able to return to Discovery High School and that a new nurse will be assigned to him.

Before John returns to school, the director of human resources contacts you by phone to inform you that he has thought about the situation and now refuses to accept the nurse from the agency for employment. He reminds you that the school site principal is away at a conference and that it would be inappropriate for a decision of this magnitude to be made in his absence.

When you request that he contact Mrs. Carlton and explain the change in plans, he refuses and makes it clear to you that it is your responsibility as the administrator in charge to make the call. You do so, and, of course, Mrs. Carlton is very upset. She proceeds to tell you that she intends to attend the next school board meeting and bring both of her sons with her, as well as a special education parent advocate and a local television news station reporter.

SAMPLE CASE ANALYSIS APPLICATION

Step 1

Summarize the case.

Mrs. Carlton is a parent with two sons who have special needs and who attend Discovery High School. She has filed a complaint because she wants a nurse assigned to one of her sons to be replaced by another nurse. You are the assistant principal charged with handling the complaint while the principal is off campus.

Discovery High School has a balanced ethnic population of students in grades 9 through 12, and the community is very supportive of the school.

The school board members visit the school often, and special interest groups have a strong influence on the board members. The school board is divided on many issues including personnel.

In response to Mrs. Carlton's complaint against a school nurse, district office personnel have been inconsistent in honoring her request to hire a new nurse for her son.

Mrs. Carlton plans to attend the next school board meeting along with her two sons, a special education parent advocate, and a representative from the media.

Step II

Identify the problem in a single sentence.
Mrs. Carlton wants a new nurse hired for her son, and she is going to take her complaint to the school board.

Step III

Select significant information and place the data into the categories.
The category *People* includes customs, norms, personalities, race, gender, sources of political power, and so on. The *Place* category includes location, physical condition, demographics, rural versus suburban, and so on. *Program* includes curriculum, grade level, type of program (special education, bilingual, and so on), private versus public, and so forth.

For this case the following applies:

People
1. Mrs. Carlton is a parent of two sons who have special needs, and she is dissatisfied with the nurse assigned to one of her sons.
2. You are the assistant principal charged with handling Mrs. Carlton's complaint.
3. The school district representative has changed his mind about hiring a new nurse for Mrs. Carlton's son.
4. There is a great deal of community support through funding and volunteer work.
5. School board members visit the site frequently.
6. Various issues including hiring personnel, employee transfers, managing racial conflicts, and funding programs divide the school board.
7. Special interest groups have a strong impact on the school board.
8. Influential groups include the Latino Coalition, the Special Education Parent Advocate Group, and the 504 Disability Act Committee.
9. Mrs. Carlton is taking her complaint to the school board.

Place
1. The school district is at the center of the community.
2. There is an increase in new housing developments in the community.
3. The population of the community is growing.
4. The socioeconomic description is moderate-to-high income.
5. Seventy percent of the community is Hispanic, and the school population is balanced.

Program
1. The school serves students in grades 9 through 12.
2. Teachers participate in interdisciplinary teaching.

3. The school has many strong, special programs including those for special education, fine arts, multimedia, technology, and engineering.
4. Programs are often featured in the newspaper and on the local television station.

Step IV

Review and prioritize the data. Identify the category that contains the most significant information leading to the problem.

1. You are the assistant principal in charge while the principal is away from the school at a conference.
2. Mrs. Carlton is taking her complaint for a new nurse for her son to the school board.
3. The school board is divided by many issues.
4. Among the groups that influence the school board are the 504 Disability Act Committee and the Special Education Parent Advocate Group.

In this case, the category *People* contains the most significant information about the problem. The location and other factors related to place are not the most significant factors. Nor is the program as significant as the people even though the students in this case are enrolled in special education classes. The problems surrounding the nurse and the conflict over the nurse are the main issues.

Step V

Refer to the data in step IV to solve the problem presented in the case and to respond to the case study questions.
Mrs. Carlton, who is planning to attend the next school board meeting with a complaint, has the support of an influential group at a school where the principal is absent and the media is concerned about what happens.

Now that you have completed the process, answer the questions for the case and refer to the final steps to help you resolve the problem. Pay particular attention to the conclusion(s) drawn from the data, which will help you to respond to the questions.

QUESTIONS TO CONSIDER

1. What is the first thing you would do in this situation?
2. What do you foresee happening at the school board meeting?
3. Who do you think will be blamed for the problem with John's nurse?
4. What could you have done differently?
5. What is the best solution for John's well being?
6. Discuss the pros and cons of mainstreaming students like John and his brother.
7. What could be the real reason the director of human resources changed his mind?
8. What seems to be the director of human resources prime concern?
9. What are the legal issues involved in this case?
10. Would you contact specific board members and warn them of the upcoming event?

Suggested Activity
Research the law that applies to the rights of students with special needs, and use this information to describe appropriate steps you would take in addressing Mrs. Carlton's complaint.

Case Analysis Framework

1. Summarize the case.
2. Identify the problem in a single sentence.
3. Select specific information from the case and categorize it according to people, place, or program.
4. Review and prioritize the information.
5. Refer to the data in each category to solve the problem identified in the case and to respond to the case study questions.

Notes

Case 2

May the Best Clerk Win

George Washington Elementary School is located in the center of a large metropolitan city. Many of its students are from immigrant families who have recently moved to the area.

Because of the massive influx of students, the school has been struggling with increased enrollment. Currently the students number 1,300, but the school was constructed to hold only 700 students. As a consequence, nine portable classrooms have been added to the existing school site.

To make matters worse, the school district has implemented a class size reduction program. Because of the facilities issues at George Washington, the school district developed a plan to relocate the nine portable classrooms to the junior high school site. As part of the plan, the fourth and fifth graders will be transferred leaving more room at George Washington to accommodate the class size reduction program.

This proposal was met with some resistance from a few of the parents who were not pleased that their elementary grade level children would be attending the junior high school. However, the school district felt that this was the only solution to the enrollment problem.

As part of the plan and in support of the students who were being moved to the junior high school site, the district also transferred nine classroom teachers and one school clerk to the junior high.

Assume for this case that you are the principal of the junior high school.

THE PROBLEM

Rosa Hernandez has been a school clerk at George Washington Elementary School for the past 10 years. She has a great deal of influence with the staff and the teachers at the school. She speaks Spanish fluently and is often called on by school administrators and teachers to translate for the Spanish-speaking parents and their children.

Rosa was one of the school clerks selected to move to the junior high. Stella Lopez was hired to replace Rosa. Stella arrived at the elementary school two weeks prior to Rosa leaving.

As soon as Stella arrived at the school, Rosa resented her and began spreading rumors about Stella. This was brought to the principal's attention by one of the teachers, but when Rosa was confronted with the matter, she denied spreading rumors and said, in fact, that she felt picked on by Stella. She also accused Stella of not showing her the respect she deserved.

Two weeks later, the junior high school site was ready for the newcomers. As soon as Rosa relocated to her new office, she began calling the elementary school to complain about her new office. She said that she never should have been moved to the junior high school and that she was not satisfied with her new assignment. She added that she heard that Stella was not doing a good job and that many of the parents were not happy with her.

A few weeks later, the district sent to each of the school sites in the district federal survey cards that were to be sent home with the students, signed by the parents, and returned to the schools. It was the school clerk's responsibility to collect the cards from the students and to contact the parents by phone if they failed to return the cards to the school. Rosa was assigned this task at the junior high school.

Rosa had dealt with this process numerous times before, and she felt that she was an expert. For Stella, however, this was a new assignment. Rosa was determined to collect all of the federal survey cards at her school before Stella collected the cards at her site.

Within a short period of time, Rosa reported that all of the survey cards had been signed by the parents of students at the junior high school and returned to the school. She bragged about being the first clerk in the district to have completed the task. Rosa, of course, mentioned that Stella had not received all of the survey cards back from the parents at the elementary school.

Two days later, a parent of one of the junior high school students met with the principal. After the meeting ended, she handed a survey card to the principal. She apologized to the principal for returning the card at such a late date and explained that she had been away on vacation and had just returned.

The principal decided to file the card with the other survey cards because Rosa was at lunch and not at her desk. When the principal opened the box where the completed survey cards were filed, she discovered that a survey card had already been filed under the parent's name. She compared the signature on the card in the box with the one that was just handed to her by the parent, and it was obvious that the signatures were not the same. After taking a close look at all of the survey cards, the principal located 25 cards that she believed had been signed by Rosa.

QUESTIONS TO CONSIDER

1. What do you do with this information?
2. Will you contact Rosa's former supervisor regarding the incident?
3. What ethical issues are involved?
4. What are the legal ramifications for forging the signature of a parent?
5. Do you think the staff will support Rosa?
6. What, if anything, do you tell your superintendent about the situation?
7. Are there grounds for suspending or firing Rosa if she forged signatures?
8. How has Rosa's behavior influenced your efforts to unite the staff?
9. What can you do to improve the relationship between Rosa and Stella?
10. What can be done to ensure that the two school sites are functioning as one?

> ### Suggested Activity
> Describe how you would document this situation and present your findings to the superintendent.

Case Analysis Framework

1. Summarize the case.
2. Identify the problem in a single sentence.
3. Select specific information from the case and categorize it according to people, place, or program.
4. Review and prioritize the information.
5. Refer to the data in each category to solve the problem identified in the case and to respond to the case study questions.

Notes

Case 3

When Diplomacy Fails

The community of Brookside consists of predominately professional white-collar families who live in moderate- to high-priced homes. Warm Creek Valley School District is located in this rapidly growing community, which is situated in the northern part of the state. There are 3 high schools, 5 middle schools, and 20 elementary schools serving approximately 27,000 students and employing 2,500 teachers.

The majority of the parents are college or university educated, and an extraordinarily high number of them participate in school-related activities. The parents are quite conservative politically, and they do not hesitate to vocalize displeasure with programs or teachers of whom they do not approve. Although the parents will profess an uncompromising desire for safe campuses and strong disciplinary measures at all grade levels, many of them will fight to protect the rights of their children to the extent that they invite their attorneys to disciplinary conferences.

The oldest of the three high schools, Swaying Pines High, serves 2,600 students and is staffed by the bulk of the district's veteran teachers. Many of the seasoned instructors distrust the administrative staff, almost all of who are new to the school. The staff was displeased with the previous administrative team, but they were typically left alone to do their own thing. Some of the veteran teachers believe that the new administrators were sent to the school to clean house and to change the way things were done. Additionally, it was rumored that many of the Asian parents expressed their distrust of the way in which the former administration handled disciplinary matters with the students.

The new administrative team is comprised of competent educators. They are optimistic and energized. The principal is very knowledgeable, and his charismatic personality quiets group tension. The assistant principals have various backgrounds and bring diverse educational experiences to the team. All of them have something worthwhile to offer Swaying Pines.

Assume for this case that you are the principal at Swaying Pines High School.

THE PROBLEM

Jerry Briscoe was in his first three months as an assistant principal for the school. He had a reputation as a problem solver. As assistant principal, Jerry had developed a reputation with certificated and classified staff as an approachable and affable colleague. Student behavioral problems seemed to be Jerry Briscoe's specialty, and staff members always seemed grateful and satisfied when Jerry handled problems created by students in the classroom. It was the overall feeling of the staff that the campus was safer and more orderly since Jerry's arrival.

Jerry was put in charge of disaster preparation for Swaying Pines High School. Following one of the disaster drills, he convened a meeting and invited community members, a few of the staff, and a representative from law enforcement to discuss the drill.

Mr. Collier, a school counselor, interrupted the meeting. He approached Jerry and informed him that he had just broke up a heated argument between two students. He also reported that he had followed the primary troublemaker to a pay phone. Mr. Collier said that he had instructed the student to follow him to the office, but the student had refused. Mr. Collier reported overhearing the student making a telephone call to request some "back up." Mr. Collier was concerned that the situation would escalate. According to Mr. Collier, the student proceeded to his next class following the phone call.

As Mr. Collier was explaining the incident, Jerry knew instinctively the specific student involved in the altercation. After Mr. Collier described the young man, Jerry's suspicion was confirmed. It was the same student, Dillon, whom Jerry had met in the counseling office a few days earlier. Dillon was enrolling in school and Jerry had noticed the tattoos on his arm that signified an association with a well-known gang in the area. Jerry remembered thinking that he would have to keep his eye on this student.

When Mr. Collier finished explaining the incident, Jerry decided to invite a police officer who was at the conference to accompany him to Dillon's classroom in case Jerry needed assistance. Jerry requested that the officer wait outside the classroom in order to avoid alarming Dillon, the teacher, or the other students. On entering the classroom, Jerry observed that the teacher, Mrs. Morales, was taking attendance and the students were quietly at work.

Mrs. Morales acknowledged Jerry with a glance and a nod. Jerry explained to the teacher that he needed to speak with Dillon. He approached Dillon and quietly requested that Dillon follow him out of the classroom so that they could discuss the incident. Dillon refused.

The assistant principal was perplexed because students usually responded to him positively when he used this soft, nonadversarial approach. Several more requests were met with the same response. Jerry thought perhaps Dillon was uncomfortable because Jerry was standing so close to him. Thus, he stepped back and again requested that Dillon leave the classroom with him. Finally, it appeared to work. Dillon stood up, took a few steps toward the door and began to follow Jerry out of the classroom.

Suddenly, Dillon reversed his direction, shouted profanities, and insisted that he was not going anywhere with the assistant principal. Dillon lunged at Jerry, and, as the other students watched, Dillon attempted to punch Jerry and kick him. Jerry blocked Dillon's punch and managed to subdue him momentarily. Because of the commotion coming from the classroom, the police officer entered the room and assisted Jerry in restraining Dillon. Dillon continued to struggle. Eventually, Dillon was handcuffed and escorted to the main office.

QUESTIONS TO CONSIDER

1. Could Jerry Briscoe have handled this incident differently? Should he have anticipated it? Defend his actions or suggest a different approach.
2. Could Mr. Collier have had more of an impact on this situation?
3. Do you have uniformed officers on your campus? If so, how well does the community accept this practice? Would you have asked the officer to wait outside?
4. Would Jerry Briscoe's approach have been different if Dillon was a 120-pound ninth grader or a 200-pound senior?
5. Once the officer gained control of Dillon, what should have been Jerry Briscoe's next step?
6. Which individuals in this case should be interviewed and asked for statements?
7. If Dillon's parents bring him to the principal's office to complain about the bruises on

Dillon's arms, what steps should be taken to address their concern?

8. Describe Jerry Briscoe's role in the follow-up investigation.

9. Dillon's mother is from Taiwan. Jerry is Caucasian. Given the apparent lack of trust by the Asian community toward the past administration, should the principal intervene on Jerry's behalf?

10. What legal steps should Jerry take, if any?

Suggested Activity

List the resources available in your area that provide training for school violence intervention. Write a memo to convince the superintendent that you need one of these services for a professional development program that offers training to your staff.

Case Analysis Framework

1. Summarize the case.
2. Identify the problem in a single sentence.
3. Select specific information from the case and categorize it according to people, place, or program.
4. Review and prioritize the information.
5. Refer to the data in each category to solve the problem identified in the case and to respond to the case study questions.

Notes

Case 4

Got Lunch?

The community of Bayshore is composed primarily of white-collar professionals. It was a planned community, and the residents are predominantly upper middle class and consider Bayshore the best place to live.

The local high school, Fairfax High, has an enrollment of approximately 3,000 students. The school was built in 1992 to accommodate 2,000 students. The campus covers approximately 60 acres and is currently the only high school in the area. An additional high school is being built and should be ready for operation in 2000. When the new school opens, changes in the attendance boundary will go into effect. There is a lobbying effort in progress in response to the new boundary proposal.

The composition of the student population of Fairfax is 25 percent African American, 15 percent Asian, 10 percent Hispanic, and 50 percent Caucasian. Occasionally, there have been conflicts on the Fairfax campus. However, when students are surveyed, they report that they get along well with each other and are very positive about the school environment.

Administrative and support staff consists of one principal, three vice principals, six counselors, one attendance coordinator, and one school police officer assigned to the school. There are 150 certificated employees at Fairfax.

Assume for the case that you are the principal at Fairfax High School.

THE PROBLEM

For the past 20 years, the district has had an open-campus lunch policy. Students were allowed to leave campus during their 30-minute lunch period and return to school by fifth period. In November, the school board intends to implement a closed-campus lunch policy. The students will no longer be allowed to leave campus during the lunch period.

The closed-campus policy is not popular among the students. The principal will be responsible for enforcing a policy that the students perceive as a denial to them of their freedom to leave the campus during their lunch period. Furthermore, the thought of having to eat the food from the cafeteria is displeasurable to some of the students who claim that the cafeteria food is unsatisfactory.

In your role as principal, you decide to organize a committee composed of class representatives, select students, parents, teachers, and anyone else who wish to participate. This group will meet periodically for the next several months to develop a plan to implement the closed-campus policy. The committee's task is to address the following questions:

1. How does the cafeteria plan to feed 3,000 students in 30 minutes?
2. Where will the students eat?
3. How will the school secure the campus?

4. How will custodial services be handled?
5. How will the students occupy their time following lunch?

The following information presents portions of the minutes from the meetings as they progress.

Food Services

Currently the cafeteria has four serving lines inside the building, four serving windows, and six movable carts. The cafeteria manager stated that eight additional movable carts would be needed to accommodate the students. The newly formed committee did not think that this was enough and requested additional carts. The district denied the request.

The cafeteria manager told the committee that food services was actively looking for fast-food vendors. The group created a survey that asked students for suggestions on food items they would be interested in purchasing. In the same survey, the students were asked to vote on whether or not they wanted to start school five minutes earlier in the day and add an additional five minutes to their lunch period.

Students on the committee expressed a concern that food-service workers needed to be trained. The cafeteria manager suggested hiring student helpers. The students on the committee did not like this idea because they believed that students would not want to work during their lunchtime.

Facilities

The school is fortunate to have a cafeteria where students can eat. However, it has only 14 lunch tables. Outside the cafeteria, there are a handful of tables and a few benches with very little shade. The district agreed to provide additional outdoor tables and benches. They cannot guarantee, however, that the tables will be delivered before school starts in September.

The committee agreed to open the outdoor amphitheater, which could easily handle 800 students, as an additional eating area. The committee also approved an allocation of $7,000 to be spent on fencing to secure the campus. The issue of what to do in inclement weather was introduced as a discussion item. It was decided that during inclement weather the auditorium would be opened for students to eat their lunch.

Supervision

The group discussed the need to increase supervision during the lunch period. Unfortunately, the district could not afford to provide funds for hiring noon supervisors. The vice principals were charged with assigning supervisory responsibilities to existing staff, including aides, the administrative team, and the counselors. The committee believed that someone should be assigned to monitor the traffic at the front gate. Also, some areas of the campus would need to be closed during lunch, and the parking lot and lower athletic fields were to be considered off limits during lunch period.

The committee suggested that perhaps more than one lunch period should be scheduled. The students on the committee felt that if more than one lunch period was scheduled some students would attend both lunch periods and not attend class.

Custodial Services

The district agreed to increase the time allotted for custodians to pick up trash and clean the lunch areas. It was suggested that additional trash cans be purchased.

Student Services

The committee estimated that the students needed approximately 10 minutes to eat their lunch and the rest of the time to socialize. As a result, it was recommended that the student body submit to the committee a list of lunch period activities that would be scheduled to keep the students occupied. A suggestion was made that radios and CD players should be available to students during lunch. However, the committee did not approve this idea because they felt that this would cause more problems than it would solve.

For this case assume that you are the principal of the high school.

QUESTIONS TO CONSIDER

1. You are hearing rumors that students are planning a walkout at lunchtime to protest the closed-campus policy. What steps would you take in preparing for this event?
2. Do you believe that a closed-campus policy is a positive or negative idea?
3. You have worked hard to develop a positive relationship with local businesses. What impact do you think the closed-campus policy will have on local businesses?
4. How do you plan to address the negative comments regarding the quality of the cafeteria food?
5. If the media arrives at your campus on the first day of closed campus, how will you respond?
6. Some students are currently using telephones during class time to order food. Should this be allowed?
7. How would you organize a much-needed lunch intramural program without additional funds?
8. How do you handle an increased need for pest control services because students are eating at various locations on the school grounds?
9. Would you consider allowing certain groups the privilege of leaving campus during lunch?
10. Evaluate the minutes from the meetings and analyze the contents related to various categories. Do some categories seem to have more weight than others do?

Suggested Activities

1. Develop a plan for a committee to visit various high school campuses that have a closed campus-lunch policy in place.
2. Prepare a press release regarding the implementation of a new closed-campus policy at your school site.

Case Analysis Framework

1. Summarize the case.
2. Identify the problem in a single sentence.
3. Select specific information from the case and categorize it according to people, place, or program.
4. Review and prioritize the information.
5. Refer to the data in each category to solve the problem identified in the case and to respond to the case study questions.

Notes

Case 5

In the Wrong Place at the Wrong Time

The community of Mountain View has a population of 90,000. It is a relatively young community as compared with the rest of the county. People move to Mountain View to get away from the hustle and bustle of the city.

Mountain View High School was 5 years old when it began to operate as a 9th through 12th grade school. With a current enrollment of 2,740 students, the school is located on 92.5 acres of land and accommodates a $40 million facility containing 61 classrooms, 26 labs, and 6 classrooms specifically designed for special education students.

The school has a diverse population of 40 percent Caucasian, 30 percent Hispanic, 27 percent African American, and 3 percent Native American students. During its first year of operation, the school experienced some racial tension. However, the school culture has evolved to a point where this tension has waned. Mountain View's staff includes 111 teachers, 5 administrators, 5 counselors, 1 librarian, 1 school psychologist, and 48 classified employees.

In addition to a strong core curriculum, Mountain View offers a wide variety of college preparatory classes. All extracurricular sports are offered on site, except the aquatic programs, which are scheduled at a nearby community pool. Mountain View's athletic program, band, choir, and academic teams are all highly competitive and recognized at the local, state, and national levels for their outstanding performances.

For the following case assume you are the principal at Mountain View High School.

THE PROBLEM

Bart Smith is an 18-year-old senior with a history of mistreating women. There have been several occasions in which Bart has demonstrated inappropriate behavior particularly toward a female student named Lupe. Lupe has been described by her teachers as quiet and respectful.

Bart transferred recently from another school within the district because his family was not satisfied with the way Bart had been treated at the first school. His parents insisted that Bart was the victim of racial prejudice at his former school.

On a Tuesday morning, the assistant principal received a call from a staff member who reported seeing a male student entering the ladies' restroom.

A female campus supervisor was sent to the restroom to investigate the matter. After searching the restroom, the campus supervisor reported that she was unable to locate a male student there. Later that same period, another call was received in the principal's office from a different teacher who reported seeing a male student leaving the ladies' restroom. This time, the student was identified as Bart.

By the end of lunch period, a rumor was spreading across the campus that Bart was seen in the ladies' restroom with Lupe and that they were involved in a fight. Bart was seen hitting Lupe and knocking her to the ground.

As a result of the rumor and after having received the two calls reporting that Bart was in the ladies' restroom, you decided to send for Bart and Lupe.

Within a few minutes, both of the students arrived at your office and waited for you to meet with them. In the meantime, the parents of both students had been contacted and they also were waiting to meet with you.

While all of this was taking place, one of Lupe's girlfriends was in the counseling office informing one of the school counselors that Lupe told her that she had been beaten by Bart on many occasions. In fact, according to Lupe's friend, Bart had broken Lupe's hand, and Lupe had told her parents that she had fallen down at school. Lupe's friend informed the counselor that Bart had threatened Lupe's life and that she was afraid for Lupe.

The school counselor shared this conversation with you just before you were to meet with Bart, Lupe, and their parents.

QUESTIONS TO CONSIDER

1. How would you approach the supervisor who failed to find Bart and Lupe in the ladies' restroom?
2. Was there adequate supervision to prevent this incident from occurring?
3. How would you respond to the school counselor after she informed you of the conversation between herself and Lupe's friend?
4. What information should be released to the staff concerning this incident?
5. Who should be notified regarding this incident besides the parents of the students involved?
6. What problems do you anticipate from the parents?
7. At what point do you notify the district office?
8. How do you respond to the media if they contact you?
9. What disciplinary action is appropriate, if any?
10. Should there be any counseling service provided to the students? If so, what kind?

Suggested Activity

Determine how you would respond if a television reporter and a camera crew came onto the campus at the end of the school day and started interviewing students regarding the incident.

Case Analysis Framework

1. Summarize the case.
2. Identify the problem in a single sentence.
3. Select specific information from the case and categorize it according to people, place, or program.
4. Review and prioritize the information.
5. Refer to the data in each category to solve the problem identified in the case and to respond to the case study questions.

Notes

Case 6

Reclaiming Rose Place

Rose Place is a middle-class community that has been engaged in the development of a new low-income housing project. During the past 50 years, it has been the home of influential white supremacists. This group frequently protests changes in the community and has recently voiced dissatisfaction with the low-income housing project. They have expressed concern about the potential problems they believe newcomers will bring to the area.

Even though it was believed that many of the original white supremacy members migrated to regions elsewhere in the nation, they left behind many children and grandchildren who have been influenced by their ancestors.

Smith-Jackson is a 40-year-old elementary school located just north of the center of town. It has an enrollment of 600 students, 20 of which are special-needs students who require classrooms with special access to accommodate their physical handicaps. The community is proud of this program and many of the parents in the area volunteer to help the physically handicapped students at Smith-Jackson.

In addition to these students who are bused to the elementary school, the school district has adopted a voluntary busing program that encourages underrepresented students to enroll in the school. This is the district's attempt to integrate Smith-Jackson in response to the state's mandate that all schools be integrated by the end of the decade.

In spite of the community's acceptance of the busing program that brings special education students to Rose Place, there is a strong and vocal group of parents who object to the busing of students who are ethnically different from the majority of the population in the community to the elementary school. According to some individuals, "If they aren't white, they aren't right." This same group of parents is quick to point out to the school board that a number of the students who participate in the voluntary busing program are experiencing problems at school and do not seem to be keeping up with the other students academically.

The principal of Rose Place was hired recently and is the first minority administrator in the school district. Previously, he had a successful career as an administrator in inner-city schools, and he had a reputation for working well with the school superintendents. The principal was referred to the school board by the mayor of the city, who knew the principal. The mayor mentioned to the president of the school board that it would be politically advantageous if Rose Place hired a principal that the mayor recommended.

The staff at Smith-Jackson Elementary School is 100 percent Caucasian, which presents another problem for the students who use the voluntary busing program. A few of the students have expressed their opinion to the principal that they wished more of the teachers had the same background as they do.

For this case, assume that you are the newly hired principal and that your ethnicity matches that of many of the students who are in the voluntary busing program.

THE PROBLEM

A number of children who ride the bus and participate in the voluntary busing program have academic and disciplinary problems at school. Some of the teachers have expressed to you how pleased they are to have someone of your ethnicity at the school so that you can relate to the newcomers. Parents of students who are bused see you an advocate not only for their children, but also for themselves.

During one of the school meetings community members were invited to attend, a parent raised the issue of losing funding for the next school year because of a decline in the projected number of students who planned to attend Smith-Jackson the next school year. She reported that a recent parent survey indicated that 75 percent of the students currently enrolled in the voluntary busing program did not plan to attend Smith-Jackson the following school year.

One of the parents, who had lived in Rose Place for many years and was the son of the former white supremacy group's president, responded to the issue by stating that he thought the school was better off without the voluntary busing program. He added that many of the students that came to Smith-Jackson from outside of the community caused trouble at school and did not do well academically. He also said that he thought things were much better before the government stepped in and tried to change Rose Place by integrating Smith-Jackson.

Several days later, you met this same parent outside the classroom where he served as a parent volunteer. After you greeted him, he stated, "I don't have to talk to you, you know. This is a free country, and I wish you and your kind would just go back where you came from. Why don't you leave and take the students who look like you with you."

QUESTIONS TO CONSIDER

1. What is your initial reaction to the parent?
2. What insights do you gain from this experience about some of the community's opinions about the voluntary busing program?
3. What is your role and responsibility to the students in the community? To the students who are bused?
4. How do you go about gathering information on the feelings and experiences of the students who are bused?
5. How do you monitor race and human relations at your school?
6. Should you inform the superintendent of your encounter with the parent?
7. Does the parent have a legitimate concern?
8. How will you address his concern regarding the students who are bused to Smith-Jackson?
9. Should you plan a race relations development day for your staff?
10. What is your district's policy on hate crimes?

Suggested Activity
Develop a plan for creating a forum to address race relations in your community.

Case Analysis Framework

1. Summarize the case.
2. Identify the problem in a single sentence.
3. Select specific information from the case and categorize it according to people, place, or program.
4. Review and prioritize the information.
5. Refer to the data in each category to solve the problem identified in the case and to respond to the case study questions.

Notes

Case 7

Whose Problem Is It Anyway?

The community of Willowcreek was originally a rural community with a rich history of farming and cattle ranching. Over time, it has grown into a suburban community with an average annual household income of $35,000.

A study conducted in 1996 indicated that two-thirds of the students lived in single-family dwellings and one-third came from multiple-family apartments and condominiums. Seventeen percent of the district's students receive financial aid in the form of Aid to Families with Dependent Children (AFDC). There are seven elementary schools for kindergarten through fifth grade students in the district that teach from 250 to 540 students per school.

Creekside is one of the two middle schools in the district. It has 720 students. It was built in 1923 and was originally the only school that taught kindergarten through twelfth grade in the community before it became a middle school. Six portable structures have been added to the existing school. Four years ago, with federal funding, the original building and all of the offices were modernized with new floors, carpets, and windows.

The staff consists of 34 classroom teachers, including 3 special day-class teachers and 1 teacher for students who are severely handicapped. In addition, there is one vice principal and one counselor. The staff is highly educated, and 82 percent of the teachers possess a master's degree. During the past two years, a technology grant allowed for the construction of a computer lab and the purchase of an additional computer for each classroom.

For the following case, assume that you are the principal at Creekside Middle School.

THE PROBLEM

Willowcreek has a reputation for its intolerance of cultural diversity. Recently, a controversial and long awaited housing project for families of Navy personnel was completed. During the summer, 20 children who were scheduled to attend the middle school moved into the Navy housing and enrolled in Creekside Middle School. Eighteen of the twenty students were African American.

When these students started school in September, they spent most of their time together during lunch and walked with each other during the passing periods between classes. Two of the female students from this group referred to their friends as their "homegirls," and they often wore clothes with similar colors. As a result of their unusual appearance and behavior, the other students on campus began to make fun of them and call them names.

By the end of October, the vice principal and counselor had met with several groups of students on various occasions to discuss plans to dissolve the ongoing tension. During the next two months, numerous fights occurred between students from various ethnic groups, and problems between students began increasing at a rapid rate. In each of the incidents, students were suspended for issuing threats, fighting, harassing, and causing physical injury to their peers.

A particular problem arose when the parents of several of the African American students demanded that the school and the school district protect their children from racially motivated harassment. They had contacted various activists from the community outside of Willowcreek to present their complaints to the district and demand peace.

QUESTIONS TO CONSIDER

1. What is the first step you can take in bringing peace to your campus?
2. What information should you provide to the superintendent?
3. What consequences are appropriate for continued fighting and/or harassment on your campus?
4. What approach will you take in addressing the parent complaints?
5. If you see that a parent is hostile or becoming hostile, what are some strategies you can implement to defuse the situation?
6. What are the legal and ethical issues involved in this case?
7. Do you think establishing a human relations committee to study the problem would help the situation?
8. What long-range plans are needed at your school to remediate this situation?
9. How would you present your long-range goals to the superintendent and to the school board?
10. What outside agencies might be helpful to achieve your long-range goals?

Suggested Activity

Investigate diversity training used in other districts of comparable size and demographics to your district, and design a staff development plan to include diversity training.

Case Analysis Framework

1. Summarize the case.
2. Identify the problem in a single sentence.
3. Select specific information from the case and categorize it according to people, place, or program.
4. Review and prioritize the information.
5. Refer to the data in each category to solve the problem identified in the case and to respond to the case study questions.

Notes

Case 8

When Students Take Matters into Their Own Hands

Rockbed is a suburban community in southern California. It consists of residential housing including single-family dwellings, apartments, and condominiums. There is virtually no industry in the area. The businesses in the community include supermarkets, restaurants, fast-food establishments, and other service-type shops.

Dry Creek Middle School is located in the center of the community and educates students that are enrolled in seventh and eighth grade. The staff at the school consists of 14 regular education teachers, 1 principal, 1 vice principal, 1 special education teacher, and a part-time psychologist. The clerical staff includes two administrative assistants, a health clerk, a media clerk, and a custodial staff of two.

The school was built five years ago, and the staff has developed a close relationship over the years. Because of the small number of students enrolled at Dry Creek, scheduling is a challenge, but the staff has worked in harmony to meet this challenge in order to provide a quality program for its students.

The faculty who teach at Dry Creek are dedicated. Mr. Lincoln and Mrs. Washington teach eighth grade language arts and history, respectively. Mr. Molecule teaches eighth grade science and Ms. Digits, who is the most popular teacher at Dry Creek, teaches math. Mr. Caesar and Mrs. Grammar teach seventh grade language arts and social studies classes, and Mr. Einstein teaches seventh grade math.

The students assigned to special education classes meet with Mr. Sped during the first four periods of each day and are enrolled in elective classes for the last two periods of the school day. The regular education teachers work well with Mr. Sped in sharing the responsibility of offering quality programs and services to the special education students.

During the current school year the number of students enrolled in the seventh and eighth grade vary considerably. There are only 110 students enrolled in the 7th grade, whereas there are 160 students enrolled in the 8th grade. The difference in the number of students presents a challenge for the principal at Dry Creek, who worked hard with the staff to prepare a schedule that would be supported by all of the teachers.

At the beginning of the school year the principal asked a few of the seventh grade teachers to teach the eight grade and because of the team spirit and cooperative working environment at Dry Creek, the teachers agreed to make the change for the sake of the students. This was typical of Dry Creek teachers.

For this case, assume that you are the principal at Dry Creek Middle School.

THE PROBLEM

By the middle of the school year, another middle school in the school district, Baxter Middle School, experienced significant growth because of the completion of a new housing development in the community.

The superintendent was receiving pressure from the parents of the students enrolled at Baxter Middle School to reduce the number of students in each class and increase the number of teachers in the school. The superintendent decided to transfer one of the teachers from Dry Creek Middle School to Baxter in the middle of the school year in response to the pressure from the parents of Baxter's students.

When transfers of teachers are necessary, the district policy states that the teacher(s) who will be transferred are the ones with the least seniority. Ms. Digits has the least seniority at Dry Creek and, the superintendent chose to transfer Ms. Digits to Baxter.

The solution to Baxter's enrollment problem was good for Baxter but not good for Dry Creek. When the teachers at Dry Creek discovered the superintendent's plan to transfer Ms. Digits, they met with you, the principal, to make known their objections. You explained to the teachers that you already voiced your concern to the superintendent, but she informed you that her mind was made up and that she was following the district's transfer policy.

The teachers are not satisfied with your response to their concern, and they select a few representatives to meet with the superintendent over your objection.

At the meeting with the superintendent, the teachers inform the superintendent that Ms. Digits is a valued faculty member at Dry Creek, and they implore her not to transfer Ms. Digits. The superintendent ignores their pleas, directs them to leave her office, and orders them back to Dry Creek.

The teachers return to their school and begin to share with the students the fact that Ms. Digits will be transferred to Baxter. When the students discover the superintendent's plan to transfer one of their favorite teachers, they decide to take matters into their own hands.

At approximately 8:00 A.M. on a Monday morning you receive a phone call from the superintendent who informs you that there are at least 60 students marching in front of the district office along with about 30 parents who have joined the students to protest Ms. Digit's transfer. She instructs you to report to the district office as soon as possible to remediate the situation. She adds that if the students and the parents are not dispersed from the district office by 9:30 A.M., you can look for a new job.

You immediately leave your office. You stop by Mr. Sped's classroom to invite him to accompany you to help with the dispersion of the students and parents at the district office. You discover that Mr. Sped is not in his classroom. Instead, his instructional aide is sitting at his desk, and she informs you that she is planning on teaching Mr. Sped's class because Mr. Sped is leading the demonstration at the district office.

QUESTIONS TO CONSIDER

1. How do you handle the situation at this point?
2. What is your opinion of the manner in which the superintendent dealt with the teachers who met with her to express their concern about Ms. Digit's transfer?
3. What factors in this case made it difficult for the teachers to accept the superintendent's decision?
4. What steps will you take to defuse the volatile situation?
5. What responsibility does the school have for the behavior of its students when they are off school grounds?
6. How do you deal with the parents who are involved in the protest?
7. The school day does not start until 8:30 A.M.; what can you do to keep other students from going to the district office and joining the protest?
8. What consequences should the students who are participating in the protest face?
9. Are you and the district office liable for any injury that might occur to the students who are participating in the demonstration?
10. What actions will you take in addressing the issue of the teacher who led the protest?

Suggested Activity

Prepare a report for the superintendent. Explain how you dispersed the students at the district office and brought them back to school.

Case Analysis Framework

1. Summarize the case.
2. Identify the problem in a single sentence.
3. Select specific information from the case and categorize it according to people, place, or program.
4. Review and prioritize the information.
5. Refer to the data in each category to solve the problem identified in the case and to respond to the case study questions.

Notes

Case 9

No Matter What, It Isn't Working

The community of Castletown is extremely supportive of its high school, Montclair High. Many parents in the community attended Montclair in their youth and remain involved in school activities, especially those related to athletics. Parental input is ongoing and influential. Community members do not hesitate to contact school board members about various issues, including some that may be considered irrelevant. The composition of the student population at the high school has remained stable for the past five years. Although the teaching staff is primarily Caucasian, many of the teachers speak Spanish fluently.

Montclair High School is the only comprehensive high school in a 175-square-mile region. It serves a large, semirural unincorporated area. It has an enrollment of 1,900 students with a teaching staff of 90, including 6 special education teachers. There are three assistant principals, three counselors, a part-time athletic director, and a fairly large clerical staff.

The school district is facing a bond election this year. The administration needs the support of the community in order to pass this bond. Many classified employees work in this district, and the school district needs the vote of every citizen. Serious problems exist with the classified staff at the site, and the previous administrator resigned because of unresolved issues dealing with the evaluations of classified employees who had been at the high school for a long time.

For the following situation, assume you are a first-year principal at Montclair High School.

THE PROBLEM

This school year the district hired a new school counselor, Steve Morris, to fill a vacated position at Montclair High School. The previous counselor retired after serving the high school for almost 30 years. Steve was hired one week before school started and had little or no training for the job. His primary responsibility was to help students with their academic schedules.

Steve's outgoing personality, positive attitude, and hands-on approach was in direct contrast to the previous counselor's style. During Steve's first week in the position, Martha, a member of the classified counseling staff, commented on Steve's approach to students and alluded to his familiarity with them. This included placing his hands on their shoulders or patting them on the back. She became increasingly agitated when she saw him hug a student in his office. During lunch she would share her observations with the other female classified staff in the office. Soon, all of the classified staff were making comments concerning Steve's behavior.

Steve's lack of experience in academic counseling and his unfamiliarity with the computer software system caused him to make several serious mistakes in student scheduling. Martha chastised him in front of students for his errors. Following one of these episodes, Steve approached Martha, placed his hands on her shoulders, and instructed her to calm down. She immediately contacted you to express her displeasure with Steve's actions. She also commented that Steve was making serious mistakes in student scheduling and in his record keeping.

As the principal, you are extremely cautious in dealing with Martha because you are aware of her history of problems with the former principal. Two years ago, the previous administrator gave Martha a poor evaluation. He removed her from the counseling staff and placed her in the library. Martha took her complaint to the classified union, which resulted in a series of meetings with district level administrators.

To further complicate the issue, Martha is claiming that several female students personally have told her they do not like Mr. Morris to touch them. She also claims that parents are calling the other school counselors to complain about Steve's scheduling mistakes. You decide to conduct numerous interviews with classified staff, who confirm what Martha has shared with you.

QUESTIONS TO CONSIDER

1. What do you do now?
2. What are your legal and ethical considerations?
3. What role do unions play in this matter?
4. Is it a good idea to require written statements from the people involved?
5. What is your opinion of Martha's actions? Mr. Morris' actions?
6. What concerns do you have regarding employees who have a strong voice in school matters?
7. Should you inform the superintendent of these concerns?
8. How do you proceed if you discover that Martha is not telling the truth?
9. How do you proceed if you discover Martha is telling the truth?
10. How might this effect the bond election?

Suggested Activity

Research the Supreme Court's ruling addressing a school district's responsibility regarding sexual harassment in the workplace.

Case Analysis Framework

1. Summarize the case.
2. Identify the problem in a single sentence.
3. Select specific information from the case and categorize it according to people, place, or program.
4. Review and prioritize the information.
5. Refer to the data in each category to solve the problem identified in the case and to respond to the case study questions.

Notes

Case 10

Lice Aren't Nice: Parents Can Be Worse

Dodgetown is a community in southern California, which is rich in cultural, racial, and economic diversity. It cherishes its variety of cultural backgrounds and celebrates high expectations for the children who live in Dodgetown. The school district consists of 10 elementary schools that provide educational services to students in kindergarten through sixth grade.

At Silver Bullet Elementary School, the staff consists of 33 teachers and 13 instructional aides. The population's ethnic distribution includes 52 percent Caucasian, 30 percent Hispanic, 14 percent African American, 2 percent Native American, 6 percent Asian, and 5 percent Pacific Islander students. Silver Bullet is 1 of 10 schools in the district that qualifies for Title I funds with 94 percent of the student population qualifying for free or reduced-cost lunches. The school also serves as a center for students with limited English-speaking ability, and it provides instruction to 203 students who are not fluent in English. The parents, administration, and staff are committed to the principle of celebrating life through learning.

For the following case, assume that you are the assistant principal of Silver Bullet Elementary School.

THE PROBLEM

On a Monday morning, Starley Night, a first grade student at Silver Bullet, arrived at the nurse's office for a routine check for head lice. This was becoming a ritual for Starley. Mona, the school nurse, had again found nits in Starley's hair. Mona telephoned Starley's mom, Ms. Night, and requested that she come to school to pick up her daughter and take care of the problem. When Ms. Night arrived at Mona's office to pick up Starley, she became angry and started yelling at Mona.

You heard the commotion coming from the nurse's office. You approached the parent to calm her down but you were unsuccessful. Ms. Night informed you that it was the school's fault that her daughter was infested with lice, and she yelled at you and physically assaulted you by striking you on the shoulder. Following this incident, Ms. Night left the school and you notified the police to report the altercation.

On the following day, Starley returned to school. Not surprisingly, she was still infested with head lice and Mona knew that the parent had to be contacted. Mona asked you to contact the parent. When you contacted Ms. Night, she was very upset and informed you that she intended to personally contact the school district and file a complaint against Mona and the school district.

Ms. Night called the district office that evening and left a message for the superintendent. She ended her phone call by issuing a bomb threat and stating, "I plan to blow up the whole place and take the school nurse along with the lice-infested students at Silver Bullet down with the building."

45

The superintendent notified the Dodgetown police department after listening to Ms. Night's message. Ms. Night was immediately taken into custody, and, after a brief trial, she was found guilty of a first offense felony. She was sentenced to 3 months in jail and 90 days of community service.

Three months later, you walked into the teacher's lounge and found Ms. Night working as a volunteer in your school in order to satisfy her community service sentence. To your dismay, the superintendent informed you that you have been assigned to monitor her behavior while she is at your school and fulfilling her community service sentence.

QUESTIONS TO CONSIDER

1. How do you handle a parent who becomes verbally abusive toward one of your employees?
2. Are parents correct to blame the school for the spread of head lice?
3. What steps should be taken to guarantee that the school is taking all precautions to stop the infestation?
4. What is your reaction to the bomb threat?
5. If Starley returns to school with nits, are you obligated to require Mona to "nit-pick" until all the nits are removed from Starley's hair?
6. Should you distribute information about head lice to all of the parents?
7. Was it appropriate for you to contact the police regarding Ms. Night?
8. Do you agree with the decision to allow Ms. Night to serve her community service sentence at your site? Why? Why not?
9. Is it appropriate for Ms. Night to return to your school in the future?
10. What type of relationship should you have with Ms. Night following this incident?

Suggested Activities

1. Review your school district's policy on head lice.
2. Review your school district's policy on bomb threats.

Case Analysis Framework

1. Summarize the case.
2. Identify the problem in a single sentence.
3. Select specific information from the case and categorize it according to people, place, or program.
4. Review and prioritize the information.
5. Refer to the data in each category to solve the problem identified in the case and to respond to the case study questions.

Notes

Case 11

Mistake in Identity

The Caucasian families who originally moved into the community of Wrongfella formed a strong power base. Since 1975, the population of Wrongfella has become more diverse. Currently, the population is 40 percent Caucasian, 38 percent Filipino, 12 percent Vietnamese, 8 percent African American, and 2 percent other. Community and school traditions are challenged as the community's demographics change. Many community members and some staff members at Wrongfella's schools hold onto the past and see a future threatened by the newcomers.

The main campus of Monroe Elementary School was built in 1975. However, it was not constructed to accommodate the increase in enrollment that has occurred over time. Twelve portable classrooms have been added during the past ten years. The school has 38 teachers, and most of them have been teaching at the school for more than 15 years.

Monroe has approximately 1,200 students, 300 of who are identified as having limited English-speaking skills. The parents are very supportive of the school and the parent volunteer program is one of the most active in the school district. The parents helped develop this neighborhood school, and there are strong ties between the school and the parents in the community.

Assume for this case that you are the principal at the Monroe Elementary School.

THE PROBLEM

At the end of the school day, you are in the process of supervising students. A parent of one of the students at your school approaches you. Mrs. Cast is with her daughter Elise and they are both crying.

Mrs. Cast informs you that something terrible has happened to her daughter, and she insists on meeting with you immediately in your office. You comply with Mrs. Cast's request.

After the three of you enter your office, you invite Mrs. Cast and Elise to be seated. Mrs. Cast tells Elise to share with you what happened to her on the playground during the school day.

Elise begins her story by telling you that a boy whose name she thought was Michael was saying dirty things to her during recess and touching her private parts. You ask Elise certain questions so that you can understand clearly what has occurred.

Mrs. Cast responds to your inquiries by accusing you of not supervising the children and allowing terrible things to happen to the children at the school.

You ask Elise if she was certain that it was a boy named Michael from Monroe, and she reassures you that she knows the boy.

At this point you are not convinced that Elise has identified the correct student. The only student named Michael that you are aware of that hangs around the playground during recess is a boy from the nearby junior high school whom you have personally escorted off your campus on more than one occasion.

You question Elise further by asking her to describe the boy. When you inform Mrs. Cast that you believe a junior high school student named Michael and not a student from your school approached her daughter, Mrs. Cast grabs Elise's hand and they abruptly leave your office.

QUESTIONS TO CONSIDER

1. What will you do next?
2. How will you investigate this matter?

3. Do you believe Elise?
4. What other information do you need to know?

THE INVESTIGATION

Before you leave work, you decide to telephone Mrs. Cast to inform her that you intend to investigate the matter further. You also apologize for offending her and inform her that you were just trying to do your job. You promise Mrs. Cast that you will notify her as soon as you finish your investigation. You end the conversation by informing Mrs. Cast that you will be out of the office the following day but that you will leave a voice mail message for the assistant principal explaining the situation.

You also decide to contact the attendance clerk at the junior high school to inquire about Michael's attendance record at his school. You want to determine whether or not Michael could have been at your school during the school day. The attendance clerk confirms that Michael was reported absent from the junior high school at about the same time Elise reported the student approached her.

The next day, the vice principal investigates the matter further and speaks with Elise again to confirm the name and description of the student. Elise admits to the vice principal that the student's name was not Michael but Mickey and that he was a fifth grade student.

The vice principal calls Mickey into the office, instructs him to leave Elise alone, and not to treat girls at the school in an inappropriate manner. The vice principal contacts Mrs. Cast with the update and suggests that she meet with you when you return to the campus the next day.

QUESTIONS TO CONSIDER

1. Are you satisfied with the vice principal's resolution?

2. Would you have done anything differently? If so, what?

THE PLOT THICKENS

On the following day, you meet with the vice principal to compare notes on the details of Elise's case. You are pleased that your assumptions about the student from the junior high school were incorrect. Michael may have been absent from the junior high school, but he had not been at Monroe harassing Elise. The vice principal also informs you that Elise's parents seemed to be satisfied with how he dealt with Mickey.

Three days later, Mickey's mother approaches you at the school and states that she is upset with the manner in which the vice principal interrogated her son. Before you can respond to Mickey's mother, Mrs. Cast walks over to a group of parents and points at Mickey's mother shouting, "Keep your children away from that woman's son!"

QUESTIONS TO CONSIDER

1. What will you do next?
2. What are the consequences likely to be if you tell the two parents to speak with the vice principal about their concerns?

3. Could this situation have been avoided? If so, how?

Suggested Activity

Research the issue of sexual harassment in schools and determine the appropriate steps you should take in addressing the details of this case.

Case Analysis Framework

1. Summarize the case.
2. Identify the problem in a single sentence.
3. Select specific information from the case and categorize it according to people, place, or program.
4. Review and prioritize the information.
5. Refer to the data in each category to solve the problem identified in the case and to respond to the case study questions.

Notes

Case 12

A Slip on Candy, Not Too Dandy

In the community of Stockton Heights, the ethnic majority has changed during the past 10 years from predominantly African American to Hispanic. This has caused friction between the two groups and within the schools. The African American parents feel the Hispanics have taken over their children's school. They refuse to understand why "those Mexicans" want to be taught in Spanish instead of English when they are in America. The African Americans wish the Hispanics would go back to Mexico and leave their school.

Powell Middle School is located in the community of Stockton Heights. Small businesses and single-family homes surround the school. Ninety percent of the students qualify for the free and reduced-cost lunch programs. Of the 1,200 students enrolled at Powell Middle School, approximately 65 percent are Hispanic, 32 percent are African American, and the remaining students are a combination of Caucasian and other ethnic groups.

This year, the school was identified by the board of education as one of the 20 lowest achieving schools in the district. As a consequence, the staff's morale and parent confidence in the school have declined.

Assume for this case that you are the principal at Powell Middle School.

THE PROBLEM

A dance was scheduled at Powell Middle School on a Thursday afternoon. The school site administrators were planning to attend a meeting at the district office and, therefore, would not be on the campus. The principal and vice principal were confident leaving the school site because the teachers in charge of the dance had supervised the school dances before and there had never been any problems.

Additionally, the administrators knew that because the dance was held on a minimum day, the school's security officer and other classroom teachers would be on campus while the dance was taking place.

After the dance began, a few of the African American male students invited Hispanic girls to dance with them. A group of Hispanic boys approached the African American students and told them to dance with "their own girls." The boys responded by stating that they would dance with whomever they pleased.

A few minutes later most of the students became bored, and they began throwing candy that had been provided by the parent-teacher association (PTA). The supervising teachers immediately warned the students that the dance would end if they did not behave.

During the incident, a male Hispanic student accidentally slipped on one of the pieces of candy that had landed on the floor. As he fell, he accidentally spilled orange punch on the pants of one of the African American students. A scuffle

53

ensued. One of the supervising teachers diffused the scuffle, ended the dance, and dismissed the students.

Unbeknownst to the supervising teachers, the students had planned to meet on the football field to settle their differences. Within a few minutes, approximately 50 students had formed a large circle around the group of students who had caused the disturbance at the dance. They began to fight.

A school security officer who was nearby contacted the school office to inform them of the incident. He requested that all of the male teachers report to the football field to help diffuse the situation. He assumed that the teachers would be outnumbered so he also telephoned the local police department, who arrived within minutes of the call.

Meanwhile, the school secretary telephoned you at the district office and informed you of the incident. She neglected to tell you that the police had been notified and that the security officer had referred to the incident as a "race riot about to happen".

You later found out that when the police arrived on the scene, the students were subdued and sent home. The police had not asked for any of the students' names nor did they file an official police report.

The next day, you scheduled a school assembly to speak to the students about what had happened at the dance and to remind them that this type of behavior would not be tolerated at Powell Middle School. You visited every classroom and asked the students to identify the individuals who were involved in the fight. You also asked for the names of the students who assembled at the football field following the dance.

Fifteen students were identified by other students as the students who were involved in the fight. You suspended all of them from school for five days. The 45 students who were identified as spectators were required to write letters to their parents sharing what they had learned from the incident.

The letters were to be signed by the parents and returned to school. You informed the students that if they failed to bring the signed letters back to school they would also be suspended from school.

QUESTIONS TO CONSIDER

1. Was the supervision at the dance adequate?
2. Do you agree with the security officer's decision to call the police?
3. Given the climate of the school community, what could you have done to ease the tension between students before the dance?
4. For students who did not return their letters signed by parents, how long would you suspend them from school?
5. Should all of the administrators have been off campus on the same day?
6. Do you believe the decision to require the student spectators to write letters to their parents was a good one? Why or why not?
7. Do you believe the consequences for the students were appropriate?
8. Under the circumstances, would you plan school dances in the future?
9. How could you have handled this situation differently?
10. What could you do at future dances to avoid this type of incident from occurring again?

Suggested Activity

Research the topic of race relations and develop a plan for working with the students on your campus to address this issue.

Case Analysis Framework

1. Summarize the case.
2. Identify the problem in a single sentence.
3. Select specific information from the case and categorize it according to people, place, or program.
4. Review and prioritize the information.
5. Refer to the data in each category to solve the problem identified in the case and to respond to the case study questions.

Notes

Case 13

The Custodian from Hell

The rapidly growing community of Ocean View is located on the northern coast of California. The majority of students attending the local schools reside in planned community housing developments and their parents pay a special tax to support the parks and schools within their residential areas.

Olympic High School is the newest high school in the community. It opened its doors in September of 1992, with approximately 1,000 9th and 10th graders. The school population has grown considerably and the projected enrollment for the upcoming school year is 1,875 students. It is the most technologically advanced school in the district with a state-of-the-art library and media center, a performing arts facility, and an engineering program.

Although the Hispanic student population contributes to approximately 45 percent of the student body, the number of Filipino students is growing, and the population of Caucasian students is declining. The student population represents a wide range of socioeconomic levels, but most of the students come from families who would best be described as middle class. Approximately 20 percent of the students qualify for a free or reduced-cost lunch program, and 7 percent qualify for Aid for Dependent Children (AFDC). Olympic also receives categorical funding for Gifted and Talented Education (GATE) and Limited English Proficient (LEP) students.

Assume for this case that you were hired last year as the assistant principal at Olympic High School.

THE PROBLEM

One of your responsibilities as assistant principal is to supervise the custodians. The custodial staff includes one head custodian, and six part-time custodians.

Mr. Cush was hired seven years ago as the head custodian at your school. When you first arrived at Olympic High School, Mr. Cush knew that you would be supervising him. He immediately confided in you that his past experience at the high school was problematic because of the lack of support he received from the previous assistant principal.

You were aware that Mr. Cush had not worked well with the previous assistant principal, and you were determined to develop a positive relationship with him.

After a short period of time however, it became obvious to you that Mr. Cush was not willing to work with you. He reported late to work, neglected his duties and the part-time custodians became openly critical of his management style. As the school year continued, you met with him on a regular basis to discuss your concerns and, in particular, his lack of personal skills in dealing with his crew.

At each of the meetings with Mr. Cush, you provided him with a written record of your comments concerning his performance. You included in the evaluation of his performance specific suggestions for improvement.

On a Wednesday morning, you arrived at the high school at approximately 6:30 A.M. A classroom teacher approached you with the news that graffiti had been spray painted on the walls of the school. He added that apparently the graffiti was targeted at you. The teacher encouraged you to look at it.

You immediately located Mr. Cush. He was walking away from his office and down the hall toward the parking lot. When you informed him of the graffiti and requested that he remove it before school starts, he informed you that he was not officially at work and that he planned to spend the day playing golf. He added that the only reason he showed up at work was to pick up his jacket, which he had left in his office.

You returned to your office and contacted the district office. You discovered that Mr. Cush had not informed the district office that he was planning to miss work and that he had not submitted a request for a substitute.

QUESTIONS TO CONSIDER

1. What is your immediate response to Mr. Cush?
2. What is your first course of action regarding the removal of the graffiti?
3. Is there a legal issue regarding unsatisfactory performance in the case?
4. What specific, legal facts should be addressed in this case?
5. How would you document the sequence of events involving Mr. Cush on this particular day?
6. What policies were violated?
7. Would you consult with the part-time custodians in regard to evaluating his performance?
8. What do you expect the classified union to do in this case?
9. You will be evaluating Mr. Cush at the end of the school year. What impact will this incident have on his overall evaluation?
10. What information should you provide to the district office regarding Mr. Cush?

Suggested Activity

Create a document that records Mr. Cush's behavior. Write a memo to Mr. Cush addressing his behavior and offer suggestions on what he should do to improve his performance.

Case Analysis Framework

1. Summarize the case.
2. Identify the problem in a single sentence.
3. Select specific information from the case and categorize it according to people, place, or program.
4. Review and prioritize the information.
5. Refer to the data in each category to solve the problem identified in the case and to respond to the case study questions.

Notes

Case 14

To Be or Not To Be the Substitute

The community of Alexandria is populated with individuals who are highly educated and quite wealthy. Most of the mothers do not work outside of the home, and they volunteer at the school on a regular basis. The families value education and want to be involved in the educational process. Almost all of the parents could send their children to a private school, but they are committed to making their public school the very best that it can be.

Emerson Elementary School opened 5 years ago, and its current enrollment is 425 students with an ethnically balanced student population. The staff is extremely close with one another and quite talented. The teachers, administrator, and parents at Emerson are committed to working together to meet the needs of the students.

For this situation, assume that you are the principal at Emerson.

THE PROBLEM

You were appointed three years ago to take the place of a highly respected principal. You are a young female and served as a classroom teacher at Emerson prior to becoming an administrator. The majority of the staff and parents supported your appointment to this position. A recent survey confirmed this fact and revealed that these groups believe that you make decisions based on what you believe is best for the children.

One of the third grade teachers at your school, Ms. Jeffrey, has just been diagnosed with breast cancer. She meets with you and explains that she is scheduled to have surgery next week and will begin receiving radiation treatment directly following the surgery. She shares with you the fact that she will undergo chemotherapy at a later time as part of her treatment plan. The two of you discuss her teaching options and decide that it would be best for her and her students if she were to take a medical leave and arrange for a substitute teacher to finish the school year with her students.

You and Ms. Jeffrey decide that the perfect person for the job is a substitute teacher who has just finished a long-term third grade teaching assignment at another school in the district. Additionally, this teacher, Ms. Murphy, substituted for Ms. Jeffrey three years ago when she was on maternity leave. Ms. Murphy is familiar with the curriculum and the school routine. Ms. Jeffrey mentions to you that Ms. Murphy is the aunt of one her students, but she states that she is confident that this will not present a problem. You inform Ms. Jeffrey that you intend to share with the parents of her students the fact that she is leaving and that Ms. Murphy will serve as the substitute teacher.

That same afternoon, you call Ms. Murphy and schedule an appointment with her to discuss the possibility of her substituting for Ms. Jeffrey. During the meeting you mention the fact that you are aware that her nephew is enrolled in Ms. Jeffrey's class and ask her if she thinks this will be a problem. She assures you that not only will it not be a problem, but that she is looking forward to teaching her nephew in Mrs. Jeffrey's class. You tell Ms. Murphy that she is a strong candidate and that you will contact her the following day if you decide to offer her the position.

Following lunch, you return to your office and discover that there is a message from the mother of Ms. Murphy's nephew. She requests that you call her immediately.

You contact the parent, and she informs you that she is very upset because the school is considering hiring her sister-in-law to teach her son's class. You are obviously surprised that she has heard about the possibility of this happening, and you ask her to share with you how she learned the news. You also invite her to tell you what concerns she has regarding the matter.

She explains to you that Ms. Murphy had already informed another relative that she was interviewing for the substitute position back east. She informs you that her family has taken drastic steps, including moving across the country, to break away from their relatives back east. It appears from everything you can gather that she has no quarrel specifically with the sister-in-law, Ms. Murphy, but she is quite concerned that Ms. Murphy might share information with other family members regarding her son and his family. She wants to know if you plan to hire Ms. Murphy.

QUESTIONS TO CONSIDER

1. How do you respond to the parent?
2. How much weight do you give the mother's concerns?
3. Should parents be involved in the hiring process for substitute teachers?
4. What additional information will you need prior to making a decision?
5. Should you speak to the nephew regarding hiring his aunt?
6. If you believe that Ms. Murphy is the best candidate for the job, do you disregard the parent's concerns?
7. If you decide to hire Ms. Murphy, what options could you offer to the parent?
8. Should you speak with the substitute regarding the mother's concerns?
9. What are the possible ramifications of hiring Ms. Murphy?
10. What are the possible ramifications of not hiring Ms. Murphy?

Suggested Activity
Research your district's policy regarding hiring relatives of students. Identify positive and negative consequences of hiring relatives of students.

Case Analysis Framework

1. Summarize the case.
2. Identify the problem in a single sentence.
3. Select specific information from the case and categorize it according to people, place, or program.
4. Review and prioritize the information.
5. Refer to the data in each category to solve the problem identified in the case and to respond to the case study questions.

Notes

Case 15

The Hip Club Ain't Happening

The upscale community of Lake Olympus has a positive self-image. Although it is relatively new, Lake Olympus is looking forward to the day it can secede from the older, established region to become a city in its own right.

Lake Olympus has three elementary schools and one state-of-the-art high school. Olympus High School has a $46 million price tag and is considered one of the most modern and progressive high schools in the state.

The adults in the community are very supportive of local events; their only concern with the high school is that they believe there are too many students bused to Olympus High from outside the high school enrollment boundary. This situation originated because of low enrollment at the high school when it first opened and because surrounding school districts needed to reduce their overcrowded high schools.

The community is convinced that any problems at Olympus High are caused by students who are bused in from the surrounding communities.

Assume for this case that you are the principal at Olympus High School.

THE PROBLEM

Olympus High School prides itself in meeting the needs of all of its students. The school promotes student participation in campus clubs and activities. It claims that more than 95 percent of the students at Lake Olympus enjoy membership in student clubs. Many of these clubs are sponsored by community organizations.

Sheila Mentor, who is a junior at Olympus High, is one of the students who is transported to the school from outside the immediate school community. On numerous occasions she has expressed her frustration with the school's policy on how clubs can be formed and who can join them. It was this frustration that influenced Sheila to form the "Hip Dance Club."

In order to form a club, the school requires that a teacher volunteer to sponsor the club. Sheila is on good terms with Ms. Johnson, who teaches sex education classes at the high school. She likes Sheila and has always appreciated Sheila's enthusiasm and highly spirited personality. She readily agreed to sponsor what she thought was a dance club.

Sheila quickly recruited 10 of her friends and her younger sister to join as club members. She filled out all the required forms and submitted them to the office.

Sheila and the club members held meetings during lunch period in Ms. Johnson's classroom. Unfortunately, Ms. Johnson could not attend many of the meetings. She had complete trust in Sheila and had no problem with the club using her classroom.

Sheila and the club members developed a secret initiation into the Hip Dance Club that required prospective members to engage in a sexual act with members of the school's football team. When Sheila's sister approached one of the football players and suggested that he participate in a sexual act with her so that she could join her sister's club, the football player immediately reported the incident to you.

On the day following the incident, you receive a telephone call from one of the major land developers in the area. He is the parent of the football player who was approached by Sheila's sister. The father informed you that he did not want you to make a big deal about the incident and told you to take care of the matter.

You contact Sheila's parents and inform them that Sheila is suspended from school for creating the initiation requirement for the Hip Dance Club, you tell them that Sheila will be transferred to a nearby school in another district. Sheila's parents inform you that they support your decision as long as the situation is handled in a manner fair to all the parties involved. However, the next morning Sheila's parents appear at school with a reporter from the local newspaper. The parents inform you that their daughter was innocent of the charges, and they want you to apologize to Sheila and her sister.

QUESTIONS TO CONSIDER

1. As the principal, what is your first step in addressing the problem?
2. When will you discuss this matter with Ms. Johnson?
3. How will you address the problem of supervision for clubs at your school?
4. How do you deal with Sheila's sister?
5. What do you do when the reporter shows up at your school with Sheila's parents?
6. How do you respond to the football player's father, who contacted you regarding his son's involvement in this incident?
7. At what point do you contact the district office?
8. How do you handle the situation when the community discovers the incident?
9. Do you approach the other members of the Hip Dance Club? What will you tell them?
10. Do you believe that removing Sheila from the school will influence the community's support for school clubs?

Suggested Activity

Prepare a letter of reprimand to Ms. Johnson for her lack of supervision for the Hip Dance Club.

Case Analysis Framework

1. Summarize the case.
2. Identify the problem in a single sentence.
3. Select specific information from the case and categorize it according to people, place, or program.
4. Review and prioritize the information.
5. Refer to the data in each category to solve the problem identified in the case and to respond to the case study questions.

Notes

Case 16

The Parent Who Ran Away with the Child

In the Stanton Unified School District, parents play an important role in the intellectual, social, and personal growth of their children. Workshops and classes are provided by each school in the district to help parents develop skills so that they can assist their children with school-related objectives. Additionally, parents are encouraged to participate in a wide variety of school activities.

Kanner Elementary School is considered by the parents of Kanner's students to be the best elementary school in the district. Sixty-five percent of the students come from a variety of ethnic backgrounds and the remaining 35 percent are Caucasian. The school is proud of its rich diversity, and many families have lived in the community all their lives.

Approximately 95 percent of Kanner's kindergarten through fifth grade students are eligible to receive free or reduced-cost meals. The school is situated in a low-income urban neighborhood and is approximately 60 years old.

For this case, assume you are the principal of Kanner Elementary School.

THE PROBLEM

You began your assignment as the principal of Kanner Elementary School two years ago, and you are a first-time administrator. The previous principal was on the site for 22 years and was well respected by staff and parents. As a new administrator, you are striving to implement a newly revised educational plan and you take pride in working in harmony with parents to achieve this goal.

Recently, a new second grade student named Tyson enrolled at Kanner Elementary School. Tyson transferred from a nearby private school, and it is immediately apparent to Tyson's teacher that he is experiencing problems adjusting to his new classroom. After just one week at school, Tyson's teacher informs you that Tyson is having difficulty sitting still, concentrating in class, and following directions. Tyson's teacher is visibly upset and asks you for suggestions on how to handle Tyson.

You decide to contact the principal at Tyson's former school and speak with her about Tyson's behavior to determine if he has had previous problems in school. She hesitates to respond to your questions at first but then offers the following information:

1. Tyson had been referred to the school psychologist for his uncontrollable classroom behavior, but his parents removed him from the school before the psychologist could assess Tyson.
2. Tyson's former principal had been informed by Tyson's parents that a neurologist had seen Tyson and diagnosed Tyson as having Attention Deficit Hyperactivity Disorder (ADHD). The psychologist also had recommended that Tyson be placed on medication.

3. Tyson's former teacher had placed Tyson on a behavior modification plan, but his behavior had not improved.

Following the conversation with Tyson's former school principal, you contact Tyson's parents to arrange a conference with them and Tyson's teacher. You are only able to speak with Tyson's father and he offers the following information regarding Tyson:

1. Tyson was not successful at his previous school because Tyson's teacher had not shown Tyson's parents any respect.
2. Tyson will not be given any medication no matter who recommends that Tyson be placed on medication.
3. Tyson is behind in reading and math because he was often sent to the "fun center" at his previous school instead of being forced to remain in class and work.
4. Tyson's father informs you that he had problems when he was a child in school and that he was placed in special classes, none of which he felt had done him any good.
5. He stated that he would speak with his wife about coming to the school for a conference. He also informed you that she would agree with him that if Tyson was having problems at Kanner Elementary School then it would be better for Tyson if he was transferred to another school in the district.

QUESTIONS TO CONSIDER

1. How will you respond to Tyson's teacher?
2. What immediate intervention should be used by Tyson's teacher to address his problems in the classroom?
3. Is it appropriate for the neurologist to recommend medication for Tyson?
4. What can you do to develop the trust of Tyson's parents?
5. What additional information should be elicited from Tyson's parents?
6. What should happen immediately to help Tyson succeed in school?
7. Should you contact the school psychologist at Tyson's former school and speak with her about Tyson's behavior?
8. Would Tyson qualify for assistance under Section 504 of the Rehabilitation Act of 1973?
9. What, if any, ethical issues are presented in this case?
10. What information will you share with the school administrator at Tyson's next school if his parents choose to transfer him to another school?

Suggested Activity

Organize a parent in-service program that addresses how to deal effectively with children like Tyson.

Case Analysis Framework

1. Summarize the case.
2. Identify the problem in a single sentence.
3. Select specific information from the case and categorize it according to people, place, or program.
4. Review and prioritize the information.
5. Refer to the data in each category to solve the problem identified in the case and to respond to the case study questions.

Notes

Case 17

An Unwise Decision

Keller Rock Unified School District is located in a rural town in the Northeast. Situated in the traditional farming community of Ridge Mountain, as some of its younger citizens have been drawn to nearby cities that offer promising jobs and lucrative financial opportunities.

The school district has one high school, one middle school, and two elementary schools. The school board is extremely supportive of the school and of one another; its members rarely display public disagreement.

School board members usually discover problems in the schools before they are brought to the attention of the superintendent because the community is small and news travels fast.

The most influential parents in the community are known for their familiar relationships with school board members, and it is not uncommon for school board members to find out what is happening in the schools from phone calls at various times during the day, especially from the parents who are most familiar with school board members.

The superintendent has been in his position for only two years. Prior to becoming superintendent, he was the assistant superintendent of the school district, and before that, he was the principal of the middle school. He has a reputation as a strict disciplinarian and is very demanding of his staff. The former middle school principal left Keller School District to become an assistant superintendent in a different district.

Assume for this case that you have just been hired as the principal of the middle school. You are new to the school district and to the community.

THE PROBLEM

On a Wednesday afternoon during fifth period, you returned to the school site following a meeting at the district office. Your secretary, Ms. Wilson, seems anxious to speak with you. She informs you that she had to locate a teacher at the beginning of fifth period to cover a class for Mr. Brock, one of the school's most popular teachers, because he had not returned to school following lunch.

During the conversation with Ms. Wilson, you learn that Mr. Brock had informed her that he was leaving campus during lunch to return some musical instruments to the local music store and that he would be back to school prior to fifth period.

Ms. Wilson proceeds to tell you that soon after fifth period began, one of Mr. Brock's students, Kimberly King, came to her office and reported that Mr. Brock had not shown up for his fifth period class. Kimberly also mentioned that her best friend, Carrie Martin, was absent from Mr. Brock's classroom. Ms. Wilson mentioned that Kimberly seemed very upset that not only was Mr. Brock missing, but so was her best friend.

Kimberly told Ms. Wilson that she knew Carrie was in school that day because they had walked to school together, and they had been in class together during third and fourth periods.

Shortly after your conversation with Ms. Wilson, you receive a phone call from Mr. Brock who is at the local hospital. He informs you that he has been in a traffic accident. He mentions that he was not injured but that one of his students, Carrie Martin, who was with him at the time of the accident, is in serious condition. He adds that the hospital nurse has contacted Carrie's parents and that they are on their way to the hospital.

He explains that he told Ms. Wilson he would return to school prior to fifth period but adds that he knew you would understand why he had not returned because of the traffic accident.

Following your conversation with Mr. Brock and after informing Ms. Wilson that you have learned the whereabouts of Mr. Brock and Carrie, you decide to contact the school district to inform the superintendent of the incident. The superintendent's administrative assistant informs you that the superintendent is at a golf tournament and will not return to the district office until the next morning.

QUESTIONS TO CONSIDER

1. What do you plan to do next?
2. What are the ethical and legal issues to consider in this case?
3. When the superintendent returns from the golf tournament, what will you tell her?
4. Will you inform Carrie's classmates of her whereabouts?
5. Was it appropriate for Mr. Brock to transport Carrie in his vehicle during lunch period?
6. What will you say to Carrie's parents regarding the situation?
7. If Mr. Brock is found liable for the traffic accident, what will be the school district's liability?
8. How will you address Mr. Brock's behavior when he returns to school?
9. How will you deal with Carrie when she returns to school?
10. Will you leave the school site and visit Carrie at the hospital? Who will you assign to oversee the school in your absence if you decide to go to the hospital?

Suggested Activity

Plan an in-service training session for your staff that focuses on the rights and responsibilities of teachers who choose to transport students in their private vehicles during and after school hours as well as the legal ramifications of such activities.

Case Analysis Framework

1. Summarize the case.
2. Identify the problem in a single sentence.
3. Select specific information from the case and categorize it according to people, place, or program.
4. Review and prioritize the information.
5. Refer to the data in each category to solve the problem identified in the case and to respond to the case study questions.

Notes

Case 18

Cultural Clash and Curriculum Chaos

Sun Coast Unified School District is a medium-sized, suburban school district with an enrollment of 13,000 students. Some schools are comprised mostly of children from very low-income families, whereas other schools consist of families from the upper middle class. The diverse community houses the district's 13 elementary schools, 4 middle schools, 2 comprehensive high schools, and 1 charter school.

The Educational Services Department at the district office is responsible for curriculum, staff development, and all of the categorical programs. The staff consists of an associate superintendent; an assistant superintendent of instruction; a director of special education; a director of student services; and four coordinators responsible for curriculum, assessment, and categorical programs.

The district has been featured in the media recently because of a proposed bond measure that would provide funding for building additional schools to facilitate the increasing number of students who are moving into the community, most of whom are Spanish speaking. If the bond passes, three new schools will be built and many of the older ones will be modernized. Without the passage of the bond measure, the district will face severe problems with overcrowding and substandard facilities.

The Limited English Proficient (LEP) population of students continues to grow. Within 2 years the district expects that 35 percent of the students will qualify for programs designed to meet the needs of the LEP students.

For this case, assume that you are the director of student services and in charge of the bilingual program for the Sun Coast Unified School District.

THE PROBLEM

A law was just passed in the state that calls for an end to bilingual education. The passage of this law has been met with support as well as protest from various segments of the community. Currently, Sun Coast Unified School District has a bilingual program at every campus, and the district strongly supports primary language development programs. With the passage of the new legislation, the district is faced with the challenge of following the guidelines set down by the law and at the same time maintaining its commitment to the needs of its bilingual student population.

Adding to the problem, the law has been interpreted differently by various school districts in the state, and a uniform policy regarding bilingual education is clearly absent. Sun Coast Unified School District received a great deal of criticism for its interpretation of the law, primarily from the English-speaking population in the community who demanded that the district adhere to the law by ending bilingual education. This same constituency resents the idea that more schools need to be built to accommodate the Spanish-speaking newcomers.

In contrast to this group, a growing number of Spanish-speaking parents want the school district to continue to provide bilingual education for their children. The school district has a reputation for meeting the needs of its Spanish-speaking students, and, for many of the parents, this is the reason they moved to the area and enrolled their children in the district's schools.

To further complicate matters, the superintendent of the school district supports the bilingual program, but her husband, who is a classroom teacher in one of the district's elementary schools, does not support the program. In fact, he was overheard at a recent school meeting stating that he strongly believed that the Spanish-speaking students did not need bilingual education and that they would perform better in school without the program.

Recently, you heard a rumor from one of the more vocal parents in the community that a large group of parents were planning to attend the next school board meeting. According to the rumor, representatives from both sides of the bilingual debate intend to share their opinions with the school board about how the district should respond to the passage of the new law. Each group wants to know how the new legislation will affect their children's education.

QUESTIONS TO CONSIDER

1. If the rumor proves to be true, how do you prepare for this meeting?
2. What additional information do you need?
3. What are some things you could do to promote the involvement of the parents whose primary language is not English?
4. There are a few classroom teachers who do not support the district's bilingual program. How do you respond to their lack of support for the program?
5. What steps can you take in educating the English-speaking community concerning bilingual education?
6. What should be the role of the superintendent regarding the district's bilingual education program?
7. A parent advocate for bilingual education brings a flyer to your office and hands it to you. It is an invitation to parents who are interested in promoting the bilingual educational program to attend a meeting to develop a strategy for promoting their cause. How would you react? What would you do?
8. The superintendent contacts you and wants to meet with you within a week regarding the status of the bilingual program. How do you prepare for the meeting with her?
9. A principal from one of the schools in the district contacts you to inform you that a group of Spanish-speaking parents have met with him to request that a committee be formed to address their concerns regarding the bilingual educational program at his school. How do you respond to his message?
10. What information will you provide to the parents who want to know how the recent legislation to end bilingual education will affect their children?

Suggested Activity

Develop a plan for working with parents at your school who have opposing viewpoints regarding bilingual education.

Case Analysis Framework

1. Summarize the case.
2. Identify the problem in a single sentence.
3. Select specific information from the case and categorize it according to people, place, or program.
4. Review and prioritize the information.
5. Refer to the data in each category to solve the problem identified in the case and to respond to the case study questions.

Notes

Case 19

The Best of Friends at the Worst of Times

The city of San Miguel is located 18 miles east of the county courthouse. It has a population just shy of 50,000 residents. The streets are lined with trees, and ample housing is available for the friendly, family-oriented people in the immediate area.

The socioeconomic climate of San Miguel is upper middle class, and the San Miguel School District reflects the appearance and values of the community. The first school in the district opened in 1891 with 1 teacher and 14 students. Today the district consists of 11 schools educating students in grades kindergarten through 8. There have been several attempts to organize the district into kindergarten through fifth grade schools and create a middle school for grades 6 to 8. However, these proposals have not received the support of the community. Most of the parents believe that their children are safe and secure in the existing kindergarten through eighth grade schools, and they do not endorse the idea of change.

The parents have high expectations for their children. All of the schools in the district have received State Distinguished School Recognition Awards, and 5 of the schools have received National School Achievement Awards. The test scores have consistently been high throughout the district, and the district ranks in the top 10 percent of the county's school districts in terms of its test scores.

Cold Creek School is one of the 11 schools in the district. It enjoys a stellar reputation. There are no apartment buildings or multifamily dwellings within its attendance boundaries. A two-parent family with a stay-at-home mom is the norm for students at Cold Creek, and it is not uncommon for the school to enroll children whose parents also attended the school. A few of the other schools within the district view Cold Creek as somewhat elitist, and the staff has experienced increased pressure from its students to maintain its standing as number one in the district.

Each year the district publishes state test results by school and by teacher. Although the test scores remain high at Cold Creek, maintaining this level of achievement year after year has created a great deal of pressure for the teachers and administration at the school. The parents have access to the test scores by class, and they use this information to request particular teachers for their children at the school.

For this case, assume that you are the principal of Cold Creek School. At your school, there is 1 vice principal and 48 teachers on staff. You are well liked by the teachers and accepted by the community, and you feel your position is safe as long as the test scores at your school remain among the highest in the district. In fact, the superintendent has just informed you that your school ranks number one for the highest test scores in the district.

THE PROBLEM

Mrs. Burton is the most-requested teacher for second grade at your school. She is respected, enthusiastic, energetic, and child-centered. Her classroom is well organized, and she uses a variety of effective teaching techniques to meet the needs of all her students. When test scores are published, Mrs. Burton's scores are always at the top. She is very proud of this fact, and she has shared with you the fact that she hopes her performance will help her to move into an administrative position some day.

You have developed a strong friendship with Mrs. Burton during the 10 years that you have been at Cold Creek. It is not unusual for your family and hers to spend weekend days together riding bikes, picknicking, and sharing family celebrations.

Mrs. Burton shares an academic building with three other teachers. Temporary walls separate the classrooms, and the second grade teachers work in teams from time to time. Only one of the teachers gets along well with Mrs. Burton. The other two teachers view her as somewhat of a prima donna.

Toward the end of each school year, you devote a tremendous amount of time and effort into organizing the state testing schedule for students at Cold Creek School. You develop clear, written procedures that you distribute to all staff members at mandatory staff meetings. At each meeting you review the testing procedures and schedule with all of the teachers. Parent volunteers and classified employees are selected to help proctor the testing for each classroom. The proctors are responsible for picking up the test materials, supervising the testing, and delivering the test materials back to the testing center at the end of each day.

This year you decide to implement a process that will increase test security. Some of the other principals in the district have developed new test security procedures, and you decide to follow their lead. You develop a procedure that addresses the transporting of test materials from the testing center to the classrooms.

You implement a policy whereby you personally place your initials next to the name of the classroom teacher whom the proctor represents when the test materials are picked up by the proctors. You follow this same procedure when the proctors return the test materials to the testing center at the end of each day.

This year, the testing schedule was planned for an eight-day period. On Thursday of the second week of testing, and about an hour after the students were dismissed from school, you entered Mrs. Burton's classroom just to visit. You noticed that Mrs. Burton was at her desk with a pencil in her hand and an open student's test booklet in front of her. Mrs. Burton immediately jumped to her feet and used her body to block your view of her desk and the student booklets. She appeared nervous and obviously felt uncomfortable that you were in her classroom.

You immediately inquired as to why she was looking through the test booklet. She informed you that she was simply checking some of her students' answers because the students seemed to erase a lot of their answers, and she wanted to make certain that the answers appeared on the tests. She also said that the proctor, a parent and PTA officer, had left the test booklets on a chair at the end of the morning testing period. She added that she was just looking through the booklets of her best-performing students because of her concern that they finished early.

You remind Mrs. Burton that test security is very important, and you proceed to return the test booklets to the testing center. After you return to your office, you request a meeting with the vice principal to tell her about Mrs. Burton and the test booklet incident. The two of you conclude that the test security procedure had been violated and that you should investigate the matter further.

QUESTIONS TO CONSIDER

1. To investigate the situation further, you plan to speak with Mrs. Burton. When will you do this and what will you tell her?
2. How does your personal relationship with Mrs. Burton affect your decision to investigate her behavior?
3. Who else, if anyone, will you need to interview regarding the violation of the test security procedures?
4. When you meet with Mrs. Burton, she denies any wrongdoing. What do you do now?
5. Will you notify anyone at the district office that you suspect Mrs. Burton cheated?
6. What do you tell the proctor for Mrs. Burton's class, if anything?
7. What is your position regarding parent requests for teachers whose students have high test scores?
8. What do you tell the other teachers at your school about Mrs. Burton?
9. How will Mrs. Burton's behavior affect your relationship with her?
10. What could you have done to prevent this from happening at your school?

Suggested Activity

Investigate your district's policy regarding testing procedures. Determine if each school in your district follows the same procedures.

Case Analysis Framework

1. Summarize the case.
2. Identify the problem in a single sentence.
3. Select specific information from the case and categorize it according to people, place, or program.
4. Review and prioritize the information.
5. Refer to the data in each category to solve the problem identified in the case and to respond to the case study questions.

Notes

Case 20

From Rookie to Reality

Shoreline Elementary is a small school with 720 students serving kindergarten through fifth grade. Comparatively speaking, it has a much smaller student population than the other 18 schools in the district.

Shoreline opened in 1970 and has maintained a reputation as one of the most desirable schools in the area. There have been only a few reported incidences of behavioral problems, and parents are actively involved in the parent volunteer program. They take an active role in their children's education and are generally supportive of the school's various educational programs.

You were hired as an assistant principal at another school in the district, but because of an illness of Shoreline's principal, you have been asked to assume the role of interim principal at Shoreline for the remainder of the school year. The district does not believe that the former principal will return to work.

The transition for you has been relatively smooth. You simply had to accept and adjust to the additional responsibilities of the job. Your confidence, in part, comes from the training you received from Rick King, who is the principal at the school of your previous employment. He spent a great deal of time with you and shared with you the knowledge and skills he learned from watching other successful administrators in the district.

You are confident that the title "interim" will be removed if you meet or exceed the superintendent's expectations. You concentrate on being highly visible, and your hands-on approach to problem solving is received well by the staff and the community. You visit each classroom on a daily basis, carry a walkie-talkie, welcome students every morning, and respond quickly to the concerns of the parents and staff.

THE PROBLEM

After you had been at Shoreline for only two weeks, you heard that Rick King had to evacuate the students because a pipe bomb had been placed outside one of the classrooms. The bomb squad had to be summoned and what turned out to be a homemade bomb was defused. Fortunately, no one was hurt.

This incident was covered extensively by the radio and television stations and the local newspapers. The concern that this type of event might recur in the district was at the forefront of every administrator's mind.

Shortly after the incident at Rick's school, and 20 minutes before the beginning of school at your site, you walked out in front of the school to welcome the students and parents. You noticed a fourth grade student running toward you with an adult whom you believed to be his mother. The two shouted in your direction and pointed at an object that was lying on the sidewalk just across the street. After you calmed the child and the parent down, you walked across the street in an effort to get a better look at the object.

You walked quickly to where the object was located and noticed that it was near the crosswalk and appeared to be made of metal. Each end was wrapped with tape. You immediately assumed that it was another homemade explosive device similar to the one at Rick's school.

QUESTIONS TO CONSIDER

1. What is the first thing you should do?
2. What criteria, if any, would you use in deciding whether or not to evacuate the school building?
3. Would you evacuate the entire school or just the buildings closest to the bomb?
4. List the steps you would take in informing the parents of what happened at your school.
5. Do you feel that school administrators should be required to receive training in bomb threat safety?
6. What type of follow-up intervention and in-service training should you provide for your staff?
7. What are the limitations and the liabilities for school administrators in a situation like this?
8. Is there any way that an administrator can reduce the amount of media coverage for an event like this?
9. What type of report would you be expected to forward to the district office regarding this incident?
10. What impact, if any, will this incident have on your status as interim principal?

Suggested Activity

Research your school district's policy on how to address bomb threats and distribute this information to your colleagues.

Case Analysis Framework

1. Summarize the case.
2. Identify the problem in a single sentence.
3. Select specific information from the case and categorize it according to people, place, or program.
4. Review and prioritize the information.
5. Refer to the data in each category to solve the problem identified in the case and to respond to the case study questions.

Notes

Case 21

Caught in the Web

The midwestern town of Benton is nestled among low-lying hills. The people who live in this secluded area often refer to themselves as the "keepers of the dream." They have managed to preserve their past and create a cultural boundary around the town that serves as a gatekeeper to prevent the influx of high technology and new-wave discoveries that they believe could threaten the serenity of the town.

The population reflects a balanced ethnic blend of people who work well together. The community is respected for its work ethic, and the local people take pride in owning their own land. Some of the Hispanic citizens of Benton have owned land for more than 100 years, and their families maintain the land and produce wonderful crops.

Assume for this case that you are the principal of Benton High School.

THE PROBLEM

The Cruz family members are among the wealthiest Hispanic landowners. They have resided in Benton for more than 100 years. They own their land, produce bountiful crops, and have instilled in generations of children the value of learning and a respect for their heritage.

The oldest of the Cruz children is Helena, a junior in high school with a grade point average of 3.8. She is interested in composing music and hopes to obtain a scholarship and attend college.

Benton High School is the only high school in the area. There are three elementary schools and one middle school in the school district. The current high school enrollment is 523 students, and the focus of the curriculum is on language arts and math. The largest organization at the high school is the Future Farmers of America. New to Benton High School is a computer lab, which was donated by a former alumnus who graduated from the school in 1948. She designated $80,000 in her will for building a computer lab.

Helena was excited about the new lab. She knew that in order to secure a scholarship for the university she would need technology skills and a computer class on her transcript. Even though she had a computer in her room at home, she wanted to use the lab at school to write her papers and conduct research on the Internet.

You have been serving as the only administrator at the high school for the past five years. Prior to that, a teacher was assigned as the lead teacher in charge to manage most of the school affairs. You were not pleased about the construction of the new lab facility. You felt that the introduction of technology to your small campus would interfere with the curriculum already established by the teachers. Nonetheless, you accepted the donation and agreed with the school board to support the construction and implementation of a technology program at Benton High. You assigned one of the math teachers, Ms. Calmly, to supervise the lab and wished her well in developing the program. You informed her that unless there was a major problem, you would prefer that she take care of all the computer lab affairs.

Ms. Calmly set up the computer lab and recruited a few parent volunteers to assist the students. She appointed one of her most enthusiastic students, Helena, to be in charge of helping other students learn the technology.

One of the first projects Ms. Calmly assigned her students was to develop a Web page. She considered this a safe assignment and thought that it would take her students at least a semester to develop the Web page and post it on the Internet.

Of course she underestimated Helena's interest in promoting the use of the technology. Within two weeks Helena had developed a Web page. She decided that because no one else at the school was familiar with the Internet, she would post her Web page herself. In order to promote her school, Helena posted one of the weekly bulletins that you mailed home to the parents of the high school students.

Helena failed to read the entire bulletin before posting it. At the bottom was a message from you. You wrote, "We are in dire need of musical instruments and cannot hold our seasonal holiday play this year without more instruments. Please deliver any musical instruments that you no longer need to the school office as soon as possible. There is no need to call."

By Monday morning of the following week, Helena was receiving messages on her Web page inquiring about the request for donations of musical instruments. These inquiries were coming from all over the world. In addition, the school office had received 53 phone calls and 10 letters asking for information about the solicitation. Within six weeks, total strangers had donated 62 flutes, 16 French horns, 7 trombones, and 5 guitars to Benton's music department; and the Salvation Army had personally delivered 9 sets of used drums.

QUESTIONS TO CONSIDER

1. How are you going to handle the situation with Helena?
2. What steps will you take in dealing with Ms. Calmly?
3. What plans do you have for the musical instruments that are on their way to Benton?
4. What can you do to stop the musical instruments from coming to Benton?
5. What will change, if anything, in the way you communicate with your staff in the future?
6. What will you tell the school board?
7. How can you turn this into a positive experience?
8. What influence, if any, do you think the posting of the Web page on the Internet will have on the town of Benton?
9. What will you do with the nine sets of used drums from the Salvation Army?
10. How do you intend to involve Helena's parents?

Suggested Activity

Locate Web pages on the Internet that feature individual schools and school districts, and identify what you believe is the primary focus of the Web site for each one you visit.

Case Analysis Framework

1. Summarize the case.
2. Identify the problem in a single sentence.
3. Select specific information from the case and categorize it according to people, place, or program.
4. Review and prioritize the information.
5. Refer to the data in each category to solve the problem identified in the case and to respond to the case study questions.

Notes

Case 22

The Gatekeeper

Monet Middle School is located in the affluent community of La Solana. This is the school's seventh year of operation, and it serves students in the sixth through eighth grades. There are 1,049 students, 23 percent of whom attend the school through the district's Voluntary Ethnic Enrollment Program (VEEP). Twenty-two percent of the students qualify for free or reduced-cost lunch. Fifty-three percent of the students qualify for the Gifted and Talented Education (GATE) program, and 5 percent have been identified as students with special needs that qualify for special education programs.

Since Monet Middle School converted from a junior high school to a middle school in 1992, all of the students, including those enrolled in special education, have been grouped heterogeneously throughout the school day with the exception of math classes. Supplemental support services are provided during and after the school day for students who are experiencing academic difficulty. The curriculum is modified for the students with special needs, and a rigorous GATE curriculum is in place.

A large portion of the GATE budget is used to fund enrichment activities such as guest speakers assemblies, field trips, and fine arts programs for all of the students attending the school.

Assume for this case that you are the principal of Monet. In spite of the mandate to track students, you wish to keep the student body as heterogeneously grouped as possible. Your challenge is to balance this commitment with the new schedule requiring students be grouped homogeneously for the 200-minute period each day.

THE PROBLEM

A few years ago, Monet eliminated its tracking system, which placed students in classes according to their skill level. The most advanced students were grouped together, and the students who achieved at a lower level of performance were grouped together. Tracking was eliminated because heterogeneous grouping was believed to give all students the opportunity to learn at a high level. The school district believed tracking gave the lower achieving students, in particular, less chance to succeed.

The administrators at Monet believed in integrating students, and it seemed that the tracking system tended to segregate students. Since doing away with the tracking system, the students at Monet have performed significantly above the national average on standardized tests. When compared with other schools in the district, Monet always has had among the highest test scores in the county for reading, language arts, and math. This includes the test scores of students who are bused to Monet through the VEEP program.

When the transition from tracking to heterogeneous grouping was first implemented, the school struggled with the change because of protests from parents of local students who opposed integrating the Hispanic and African American students with their Caucasian children. It has taken years to bridge the gap between various ethnic groups of parents at the school.

At one time, the Chicano Federation and the Anti-Defamation League had been requested to work with the diversified group of parents on behalf of the school's initiative to integrate the students academically and ethnically. However, there still remains an influential group of parents whose children are enrolled in the GATE program who are convinced that their children would be better served if they were grouped strictly according to their performance level.

In spite of Monet's success with heterogeneous grouping regarding test scores, the school board for the district recently passed an ordinance requiring all schools in the district to implement a tracking system for the upcoming school year. The program mandates a 200-minute cluster for students who are academically similar. Students identified for the GATE program would be grouped during the 200-minute period with students who are either gifted and talented themselves or who are considered the highest achieving students in the school. Needless to say, many of the parents whose children exhibit high-academic performance are pleased with the school board's new ruling.

QUESTIONS TO CONSIDER

1. What additional information do you need, if any, to determine how to proceed?
2. What input could you request from the staff prior to implementing the new schedule?
3. How could you begin bringing the parents into the process?
4. If you decide to include some of the staff and a few of the parents, what criteria would you use?
5. Assume that you strongly support heterogeneous grouping. What ethical issues would you face in deciding whether or not to use the tracking system?
6. Would you include parents in the initial stages of the transition? Why or why not?
7. Who would you rely on, if anyone, at the district office to assist you during the transition?
8. Once you have decided on a new program schedule, when and how will you introduce it to the community?
9. Because the budget for GATE students has been used in the past to benefit all of the students, explain how the distribution of funds will change with the new tracking schedule.
10. What scheduling challenges will you face?

Suggested Activity

Draft a letter to parents in your community that introduces the new tracking schedule and convinces them that it will be beneficial to all of the students at your school.

Case Analysis Framework

1. Summarize the case.
2. Identify the problem in a single sentence.
3. Select specific information from the case and categorize it according to people, place, or program.
4. Review and prioritize the information.
5. Refer to the data in each category to solve the problem identified in the case and to respond to the case study questions.

Notes

Case 23

A Question of Balance

Westhaven is a diverse community. Several individuals within the community are quite affluent and reside on million-dollar estates. However, the majority of the students attending Walnut Creek Elementary School, which is situated in the center of Westhaven, come from modest backgrounds. Many of the students are from families who receive some form of governmental assistance, including Aid for Families with Dependent Children (AFDC).

A small number of middle-class families have recently moved to the community, and they are living in newly built, single-family homes that are located in what was once a large avocado ranch. The area is known for its agribusiness, and many of the families in the community are wealthy ranchers and farmers famous for their thoroughbred horses, avocado groves, and citrus crops.

A growing number of the students attending Walnut Creek Elementary School are from migrant families who provide the primary labor force for the local agribusiness. The ethnic breakdown of the school reflects a balanced population of Caucasians, Hispanics, African Americans, and Vietnamese. Fifty-two percent of the school's population qualifies for free or reduced-cost lunches.

The previous principal of the school served for nine years before being asked to step down because of philosophical differences between her and some members of the school board. The staff at the school includes 45 certified teachers, a lead teacher, and 19 classified personnel.

The school currently has a population of 900 students in grades kindergarten through six. Walnut Creek Elementary School was established in 1869 as a one-room schoolhouse, which is still part of the school's physical site and is used for school board and community meetings. Most of the rest of the campus was built in 1945, and various wings and portables have been added over the years to accommodate an increase in student enrollment.

Assume that you are the newly hired principal of Walnut Creek Elementary School.

THE PROBLEM

When you first begin your assignment as the principal of Walnut Creek, you discover a tightly controlled campus. The majority of the teachers seem oppressed; they have come to rely on the autocratic leadership style of the former principal. You believe that you were hired to inspire creativity in the staff and to help them develop an interest in the students and in their jobs. You also believe that this change is needed and that the school board hired you to fulfill the need.

You are told that the lead teacher at your campus was offered the opportunity to continue in her position but she refused as an indication of support for the former principal, whose contract she believed should have been renewed for the tenth year.

You asked her to reconsider the position but she declined, preferring instead an assignment as a fourth grade teacher on your campus.

One week after you were hired, a group of teachers and a few parents met with the superintendent without your knowledge and suggested that one of your fifth grade teachers, Mr. Humble, be assigned the position of lead teacher. He has been teaching fifth grade at the school for three years, and he seems to be the teachers' choice.

When you hear about the meeting between the teachers, parents, and superintendent, you decide to offer Mr. Humble the position and he accepts your offer.

One of the first assignments you give Mr. Humble is to assist you in reviewing the class lists and class schedule for the coming school year. On reviewing these data with him, you notice that all of the students with Vietnamese surnames are grouped together at each grade level.

You share with Mr. Humble your concern that the grouping of students by surnames does not represent an ethnically balanced enrollment. Mr. Humble simply shrugs his shoulders and states that this is the way the scheduling has always been done at Walnut Creek.

On further investigation, you discover that many students are placed in certain classes because of specific parental requests for placement. Apparently, Walnut Creek allows parents to choose their child's teacher. You have no objection to this policy, but you notice that there are no requests from the parents of the Vietnamese-speaking students.

In the meantime, a few of your teachers have confided in you that they feel the Vietnamese students are not given the same opportunity to learn as the other children. You bring this issue to the attention of Mr. Humble and he tells you to ignore the few teachers who complain.

QUESTIONS TO CONSIDER

1. What will you do with the information from your teachers who complained about the imbalance in the classes?
2. What additional information will you need to help you address their concerns?
3. What role do you believe the teachers played in recommending the lead teacher?
4. How will you create an ethnically balanced schedule that generates support from your teachers and the parents?
5. Is it important to implement a shared decision-making model on this issue? Why or why not?
6. How will you deal with the teachers that support the previous administrator's method of developing class schedules?
7. How would you react to the news that a meeting had occurred between a few parents, a group of teachers, and the superintendent?
8. What action do you take, if any, to develop a more collegial relationship between the lead teacher and yourself?
9. How do you plan to involve the Vietnamese parents at your school?
10. What steps would you take to develop relationships with the teachers at your school who support ethnically balancing the classes to include the Vietnamese students?

Suggested Activity

Write a memo to your staff describing how you intend to change the way students are assigned to classes.

Case Analysis Framework

1. Summarize the case.
2. Identify the problem in a single sentence.
3. Select specific information from the case and categorize it according to people, place, or program.
4. Review and prioritize the information.
5. Refer to the data in each category to solve the problem identified in the case and to respond to the case study questions.

Notes

Case 24

Golden Oldies

The community of Vermillion is located in the Midwest. Once a semirural, agricultural town, it is now home to many industrial parks and small corporations. It is quickly becoming a popular family community with several new housing developments under way.

Seven Oaks Elementary School is one of eight elementary schools in the Santa Vista Unified School District, which is located in the heart of Vermillion. It has a population of 950 students. The school was built in 1959, and it is scheduled for a major renovation in the coming year.

The rapid growth of the community has left the school district with no choice other than to implement a four-track, year-round schedule for all of its elementary schools. This schedule has served the school community well for the past six years. The community has adjusted to the school calendar, and most of the people agree that it has numerous advantages.

One drawback of the multitrack schedule, however, is that it limits the number of teachers available to teach at certain grade levels. Although the administrators at Seven Oaks Elementary School do not guarantee that a child will be placed in the class of the parent's choice, they do allow parents to submit requests for specific teachers. The district policy states that parent requests are honored as long as the site administrators are able to create classes that are balanced according to the academic ability, ethnicity, and gender of the students at each grade level.

Assume that you are the principal of Seven Oaks Elementary School as you consider this case.

THE PROBLEM

Ruby Elliot is a fourth grade teacher at Seven Oaks. She has taught at the school for the past 28 years, and many of her current students are the children of former students. She has a reputation for being very set in her ways, and the teaching credential that she was awarded 29 years ago does not require her to attend additional courses to maintain her certification.

The administrators at the school site have noticed that her teaching skills have not kept pace with current educational practices, and she does not implement instructional techniques offered at recent school site in-service meetings. Additionally, many parents have criticized Mrs. Elliot's teaching, her overbearing personality, and her loud voice.

In order to help remediate this situation, site administrators provided release time to Mrs. Elliot so she could visit the classrooms of mentor teachers in her district to observe their positive and effective teaching strategies. Mrs. Elliot also has been assigned a mentor at her own school site to assist her in developing strategies for improving her curriculum planning and classroom management skills.

Despite these interventions, there has been no evidence to suggest that Mrs. Elliot has improved her teaching skills. As a consequence, you have notified Mrs. Elliot that she will be placed on a yearly evaluation schedule.

Mrs. Elliot was very upset with this decision, and she expressed her disappointment by informing the other teachers that she felt "picked on" and a victim of age discrimination. She reminded the staff that she was obviously a successful teacher and that she had 28 years of experience to prove it!

After four weeks had passed, Mrs. Elliot still had not implemented any of the recommendations for improving her teaching style. By the end of the four-track school year, the office had received 44 requests from parents of third graders requesting Mrs. Donaldson, the other fourth grade teacher assigned to Mrs. Elliot's track, as the teacher of their choice for their child. Only 55 students were enrolled in the third grade, and none of the parents had requested Mrs. Elliot.

QUESTIONS TO CONSIDER

1. What are the most important issues involved in this case?
2. What issue needs to be resolved first? Second? Third?
3. Do you inform the individual in charge of personnel at your district office of this situation? Why or why not?
4. What criteria should you use in placing the fourth grade students in classes for the next four-track year?
5. What is your opinion of the policy that honors parents' requests for teachers?
6. Will you inform Mrs. Elliot of the overwhelming number of requests issued by parents for Mrs. Donaldson?
7. What steps can you take as an administrator to require Mrs. Elliot to implement the suggestions aimed at improving her teaching?
8. What recourse do you have if she continues to ignore your recommendations?
9. How do you address that fact that Mrs. Elliot has tenure as a teacher?
10. How will you monitor Mrs. Elliot in the future?

Suggested Activity

Research the law in your state as it relates to teacher tenure, and explain how it would influence the administrator's role in evaluating Mrs. Elliot. If your state does not award teachers tenure, explain how Mrs. Elliot's employment status might be affected by her behavior.

Case Analysis Framework

1. Summarize the case.
2. Identify the problem in a single sentence.
3. Select specific information from the case and categorize it according to people, place, or program.
4. Review and prioritize the information.
5. Refer to the data in each category to solve the problem identified in the case and to respond to the case study questions.

Notes

Case 25

To Keep or Not to Keep Samantha?

The city of Salisbury is composed of an eclectic population. The community is culturally diverse and rich in its multicultural nature. The Salisbury Unified School District is situated in the northern section of the city and currently has an enrollment of more than 25,000 students. Each of the 13 kindergarten through eighth grade elementary schools is suffering from overcrowding. Students in kindergarten through eighth grade participate in a multitrack, year-round educational setting, whereas high school students follow a traditional, school year calendar.

Olivia Elementary School is one of the 13 elementary schools. It has a current enrollment of 1,050 students, and it is ethnically balanced. Free breakfast and lunch is provided to approximately 55 percent of the student body. The school itself was built to accommodate approximately 600 students. Therefore, classrooms and playground space are valuable commodities in this overcrowded facility.

Currently there are three teachers on campus who teach students with special needs. The school is planning to add another special education class for students who qualify. Additionally, there is one speech and language therapist and one psychologist who provide services to all of the special education students on all four of the tracks. The administrative personnel include one school principal and one assistant principal.

Staff surveys indicate that they are satisfied with the operation of the school and that the current administration has been very supportive of them. The certificated and classified personnel are pleased with their contributions, which are improving the educational programs at the school. They do feel, however, that the site has undergone continual interruption because of the ongoing construction needed to update the school and accommodate its increasing enrollment.

Parent surveys indicate that they are also satisfied with the overall school program, but they too are concerned about the continued increase in enrollment.

Assume that you are the principal of Olivia Elementary School.

THE PROBLEM

Samantha Toogood is a full-time special education teacher at Olivia. She has been a staff member at the school for 2 years and has a caseload of 38 students. She has an impressive background working with special education students and is considered one of the best teachers in her field.

Since coming to Olivia, she has had numerous confrontations with the staff. She has complained extensively about one of her co-workers, and she has filed a complaint about the procedures at her site for placing students in special education classes.

Samantha has requested a staff meeting to inform the teachers at her school of the correct process for referring students to special education. She insists that the teachers are ill informed and do not understand the referral process. She also requested to use this opportunity to train the teachers on how to implement certain strategies for modifying instruction for students who need special help in the regular education classrooms.

Another special education teacher, Julie Johnson, is also at Olivia. Julie offered to assist Samantha during her first year at the school so Samantha could familiarize herself with her new assignment. After working with Samantha for six months, Julie requested to be reassigned to a regular education classroom. Julie had been teaching special education for more than 10 years, and she loved her job. She requested the transfer to a regular classroom because she no longer wanted to work with Samantha.

Since Julie's departure from special education, two new special education teachers have joined the staff. Although the working relationships among the four teachers is congenial, the school psychologist and many of the other classroom teachers continue to express concerns regarding Samantha's personal relationship with the staff.

Samantha has continued to work well with the students and parents. She has developed a reputation for having a thorough approach to addressing the needs of the students in special education and her record keeping is impeccable. Samantha will acquire tenure status if she returns to Olivia the next school year.

QUESTIONS TO CONSIDER

1. What reasons would you have for retaining Samantha?
2. What reasons would you have for releasing Samantha from her teaching assignment?
3. What would you discuss with the personnel director prior to making a final decision regarding Samantha's assignment?
4. Should you decide to release Samantha, what reasons, if any, will you give her?
5. How will you respond to the parents if they oppose your recommendation to relieve Samantha of her duties?
6. How does Samantha's poor relationship with the staff negatively impact her ability to meet the needs of the students she teaches?
7. Does the fact that there are a limited number of teachers qualified to teach special education influence your decision?
8. What can Samantha do to improve her relationship with the staff?
9. List some of the recommendations you would offer to Samantha if you decide to keep her.
10. How does the personality of your staff affect the decisions you might make regarding Samantha's continued employment?

Suggested Activity

Assume you decide to keep Samantha. Write a plan that outlines exactly what Samantha should do to improve her relationship with the staff.

Case Analysis Framework

1. Summarize the case.
2. Identify the problem in a single sentence.
3. Select specific information from the case and categorize it according to people, place, or program.
4. Review and prioritize the information.
5. Refer to the data in each category to solve the problem identified in the case and to respond to the case study questions.

Notes

Case 26

When East Meets West

The community of La Esperanza has become a mosaic of neighborhood schools with a cultural mix of Hispanics and Caucasians. The majority of the Hispanic population gradually migrated to the west side of the city, and this has caused a separation between the east and west because most of the "westerners" are Hispanic and most of the "easterners" are Caucasian.

The educational system was eventually divided as well. Over time, the schools to the west developed the reputation of having low-performing students, whereas the schools to the east acquired the reputation of having high-achieving students.

Assume that you are the chair of the Community Forum as you respond to the following questions.

THE PROBLEM

The district office and individual school sites have collided in the community because of a state mandate that all of the schools improve academically. The school districts in La Esperanza responded to the mandate by replacing school principals in the schools to the west and by promoting growth in the schools to the east. The intent was to recruit new leadership for the lower performing schools and build new schools in the eastern part of the city. This news was received favorably by those living in the eastern sections of the city.

The community to the west, however, had developed a strong bond with their schools and their schools' leaders. The people had become unified in their struggle to improve the schools and to bring success to the underachieving student population. Thus, when they heard about the release of so many of their school principals, they protested, insisting on justice.

While the decision makers in La Esperanza were busy firing the principals in the western schools and promoting new schools in the east, new residents moved into the eastern section and brought with them an attitude of elitism. As a result, friction increased between the two communities.

As a consequence, a proposal came forward from an interested citizens' group that suggested the establishment of a Community Forum. This would provide an opportunity for representatives from the west as well as from the east to meet and discuss how they could improve La Esperanza's entire school system in response to the state's mandate.

The people from the west believed that they would be given the opportunity to share their concerns and request the return of their school leaders. The women were the most outspoken of the people from the west. They had provided strong matriarchal leadership and believed they knew what was best for their children and for their schools.

The women from the west spoke as one articulated voice at the Community Forum, and they reminded the participants that they were proud of their heritage and

wanted what was best for their children. They shared with the audience the high es-
teem in which they held the school leaders in their community because the school
principals honored their culture and worked with the parents to teach the students
English in such a way as to achieve success in school. They added that the schools
were recruiting parents for night classes so that they too could learn to speak English along with their children. The women talked about the need to preserve their
native language and, at the same time, to prepare their children for an English-
speaking world.

The women asserted their desire to improve the relationship between their home
life and the lives of their children at school. They felt more parent involvement was
needed, and honest discussions between the teachers at the school and the parents
of the Spanish-speaking children was critical. One of the women spoke firmly to the
group, "Tell us the truth about our children. If they are not doing well in school, tell
us. We need to know if they are at the bottom so that we can help our children. It is
our right to know." She continued, "Bring back our leaders and let us work together
as a close community on behalf of all of our children." The audience listened and
embraced the voice of the matriarchs who spoke on behalf of their community and
their school leaders.

The women concluded that the school principals had been true advocates for the
students and the parents in the west. They spoke at the forum in the hope that the
school leaders would be returned to their children's schools.

QUESTIONS TO CONSIDER

1. How would you describe the problems
between the community in the west and that
in the east?
2. What would you do to create better
communication between the west and the east?
3. What types of leaders do you believe belong
in each of the communities?
4. How would you establish the selection process
to facilitate a better match between school
leaders and parents, and staff and students for
the schools in the west and the east?
5. Many parents from the east are planning to
boycott the future Community Forum
meetings. How would you respond to this?
6. Several of the certified staff are planning to
transfer to other schools within the district
because of the problems between the
communities. How can you work with the
district on behalf of the teachers?

7. What steps would you recommend to retain
the teachers who are interested in
transferring to other schools?
8. Rumors are running rampant in the district
regarding the Community Forum. How do
you communicate with the community about
the issues discussed at the meeting?
9. Many of the existing parent training
programs do not address the issues that were
brought up at the meeting. What
recommendations would you make to the
district office regarding this matter?
10. There has been a steady growth in the
population in the east, and many of the
newcomers are migrating from the western
part of the city. How do you explain this
trend? What affect, if any, will it have on the
schools to the west?

Suggested Activities

1. Develop a plan that addresses the polarization of parents in a community
and list steps you would take to bring the groups together.
2. Showcase an existing program at your school that brings different groups
together and has created a sense of unity among all the members of your
school community.

Case Analysis Framework

1. Summarize the case.
2. Identify the problem in a single sentence.
3. Select specific information from the case and categorize it according to people, place, or program.
4. Review and prioritize the information.
5. Refer to the data in each category to solve the problem identified in the case and to respond to the case study questions.

Notes

Case 27

Quick to Accuse

Smugville is a small community nestled among foothills. The nearest large city is about 50 miles away. The town has a population of approximately 30,000 people. The economic status of Smugville is middle to upper-middle class, and the majority of the adults in the community consider themselves professionals.

The community expects a high standard of academic achievement in the local elementary and secondary schools. The students in the schools have maintained high test scores, and high scoring seniors have been recognized statewide for their achievements.

Student discipline has never been a problem in any of the schools in the district. The school principals pride themselves in providing a safe school environment with very few problems.

Assume for this case that you are the middle school principal.

THE PROBLEM

Recently, Smugville was selected by a regional committee appointed by the governor of the state to house two group homes for delinquent youths from the inner city. Each group home would be assigned 5 children ranging in age from 12 to 14 years old. One home would be for 5 boys and the other for 5 girls. The students would attend the only middle school in the town.

After the new children arrived in town, they experienced some difficulty adjusting to their new environment and their new school. The majority of the Smugville students in the school, however, did not have difficulty accepting the newcomers. In fact, the students from the group home were pretty much ignored by the student body.

The adults in Smugville have little or no tolerance for diversity, especially when it comes to different ways that children behave. In fact, the community is very proud of its well-behaved youngsters, and it does not tolerate children who do not know how to respect adults and mind their manners.

Your background has involved working with students from the inner city, and you were looking forward to working in a community with few student discipline problems. You wanted to provide a better life for your family in a small town such as Smugville.

When you first became aware that the group homes would be established in your town, you attempted to bring together in a forum representatives from the two group homes and distinguished members of the Smugville community. The response to this initiative was a complete failure. In fact, the only individual who attended the first meeting was the custodian, who decided to stay after work to see what the fuss was all about.

One Saturday morning, just as you were about to head out for your morning run, the phone rang. It was from a representative from the local sheriff's department calling to inform you that the school had been vandalized and painted with graffiti. You decided to drop by the school instead of continuing with your plans to run. When you arrived at the school, you observed that the school office was substantially damaged. Some of the file cabinets had been overturned and most of their contents were thrown throughout the office and sprayed with paint.

A sheriff's deputy located several empty spray cans in the back of the school, which were traced back to the only hardware store in town. When he was questioned by the police, the owner of the store was quick to reveal that he remembered selling the spray paint cans to two young boys from the group home.

The sheriff's deputy and his assistant visited the group home and talked with several of the boys. No one admitted being involved in the act of vandalizing the school.

When you returned to school the next Monday, rumors were flying among the students and teachers. The PTA president contacted your office and directed you to punish the students immediately. Additionally, the superintendent called your secretary and informed her that he wished to meet with you immediately. He demands that you recommend expulsion for the students involved in the incident.

QUESTIONS TO CONSIDER

1. What procedures would you follow to investigate the vandalism at your school?
2. What procedures would you set in place to ensure that your investigation does not get out of hand?
3. How would your investigation differ from the deputy's investigation?
4. How will you handle the superintendent's request?
5. Do you feel that a separate curriculum needs to be established for student diversity at the school?
6. What do you foresee happening to the group homes?
7. Do you believe the students from the group home caused the vandalism?
8. What do you believe is appropriate punishment for vandalism?
9. Who would you recruit to help you with your investigation?
10. What steps would you take to rebuild the relationship between the group homes and the school community?

Suggested Activity

Identify the policy in your school district that would apply to school vandalism and procedures for dealing with an incident such as this one.

Case Analysis Framework

1. Summarize the case.
2. Identify the problem in a single sentence.
3. Select specific information from the case and categorize it according to people, place, or program.
4. Review and prioritize the information.
5. Refer to the data in each category to solve the problem identified in the case and to respond to the case study questions.

Notes

Case 28

Here Today and Gone Tomorrow

Georgetown Unified School District is an urban school district with an enrollment of more than 138,000 students. The district covers a large portion of the city, which includes all socioeconomic levels.

Under the direction of the school district's new superintendent, an Education Academy has been developed to support and promote what the district refers to as "high-performance learning." The focus of the Academy is to study teaching and learning and to evaluate instructional practices in order to improve achievement and enhance student performance at all of the schools in the district.

The curriculum focus for its first year of operation is literacy, and the district is committed to implementing a specific program designed to improve the reading, writing, and speaking skills of the students.

Assume for this case that you are the principal of Simpson Elementary School.

THE PROBLEM

Simpson Elementary is located in the northwest section of Georgetown. The students represent more than 30 countries and speak 34 different languages. With a staff of 34 teachers, 1 special education teacher, 1 principal, a vice principal, and additional support personnel, the school functions well.

The parents of the students at Simpson insist on a rigorous academic program for their children. Many of them are employed as university professors, professional consultants, research scientists, or technology specialists. They support Simpson's program that fully integrates students with limited English-speaking skills into the mainstream English-speaking population of the school.

Prior to the new superintendent's arrival, the district received a multimillion dollar grant from the National Science Foundation (NSF). The grant was in its second year of implementation when the superintendent was hired. The funds from the grant were distributed to every school in the district with the intention that the funds would be used exclusively to improve the science and math skills of the students.

The parents of the students at Simpson Elementary were particularly supportive of the NSF grant because so many of them were professionals in the fields of science and math. This is one of the main reasons they were so upset by an article that appeared in the local newspaper over the weekend.

According to the article, the NSF issued a notice to the school district that it was planning to withdraw its grant because the NSF felt that the district no longer had a commitment to developing the science and math curriculum. The article quoted a representative from the NSF saying that the school district was no longer meeting its obligation to the grant. Furthermore, the NSF had notified the superintendent that it planned to phase out any future funding because of his focus on reading and writing.

You have just arrived at your school on the Monday morning following the release of the newspaper article featuring the NSF story. As soon as you enter the school gates, representatives from the news media, as well as at least thirty angry parents, are there to greet you.

QUESTIONS TO CONSIDER

1. What additional information do you need, if any, before you speak to the press?
2. How will you handle questions from your staff?
3. Will you contact your superintendent? If so, what information will you share with him?
4. Do you continue to focus on the science and math curriculum in spite of the NSF decision?
5. How do you explain to the students in the science and math program that their program will not be funded in the future?
6. What do you do about future staff development sessions that are scheduled and paid for from NSF grant funds?
7. If you plan to continue with the staff development, how will you finance these sessions without the funds from NSF?
8. How do you plan to respond to questions from the parents who are angry about the NSF's decision?
9. What steps should you take in reestablishing a positive relationship with the community?
10. How do you believe the staff, parents, and community will respond to you if you support the superintendent's position?

Suggested Activities

Prepare a statement for an upcoming meeting with parents. Address the status of the NSF grant and how the withdrawal of grant funds will affect your school's commitment to the science and math curriculum.

Case Analysis Framework

1. Summarize the case.
2. Identify the problem in a single sentence.
3. Select specific information from the case and categorize it according to people, place, or program.
4. Review and prioritize the information.
5. Refer to the data in each category to solve the problem identified in the case and to respond to the case study questions.

Notes

Case 29

A Time to Reflect

Maryville is a quiet bedroom community with a rapidly growing population. Most of the adults in town work in the nearby city of Featherton and commute on a daily basis. The citizens of Maryville enjoy returning home after a long day in the city and spending time with their families and friends in this respectable neighborhood.

The residents of Maryville are proud of their local high school and consider it a safe environment for their children. Maryville High offers its students numerous activities to keep their otherwise idle time occupied. The school has an enrollment of 1,450 students with 1 principal, 1 assistant principal, an activities director, and a staff of teachers who have enjoyed a long tenure at the school.

Although the high school has a population half the size of some of the high schools in the area, Maryville High has received numerous trophies for football, cross country, and soccer.

Assume for this case that you are the assistant principal of Maryville High.

THE PROBLEM

You were born and raised in the city of Featherton. You consider yourself a sophisticated and well-educated individual. After graduating from the University of Featherton with honors and receiving your degree in business administration, you interviewed for various positions but were unable to find a job.

You had always been interested in the possibility of teaching but you were discouraged from pursuing a career in education by your parents, who felt the salary and benefits were far below what the business world had to offer.

However, as you became discouraged by so many rejections for a job in the city, you reconsidered a career in education. You decided to return to the university and complete the teacher education program.

After hearing about a teaching position at Maryville High, you applied for the position, and on the day following your interview with the high school principal, you were offered a job as an English teacher.

You were looking forward to spending your days sharing with students what you knew about the subject of English and to becoming a part of the quaint community of Maryville.

After you had been teaching at the high school for 3 years, the principal, who had been at the high school for more than 15 years, encouraged you to return to the university and enroll in the educational administration program.

You were surprised that the principal approached you regarding a career in educational administration because you had only been teaching for three years, but you followed his advice and successfully completed the educational administration program.

The month after you completed the program, the assistant principal of Maryville High took another position at a high school in the city and the principal asked you if you were interested in taking her place. You were eager to please the principal and felt confident that your experience as an administrator would be just as wonderful as your experience as an English teacher had been.

During the first month in your new position, you worked hard and took your job seriously. You considered it a privilege to receive an offer to work as an administrator and quickly adapted to your new role. By this time, you had even convinced your parents that pursuing a career in education was not such a bad idea after all.

Part of your assignment as the assistant principal was to supervise athletic activities. The principal relied on you to supervise all of the after school soccer games because he considered this valuable time for himself in taking care of school matters that he could not attend to during the school day.

One afternoon, just as you were about to leave school to help supervise an after school soccer game at another high school in the area, Morningside High, the principal of Morningside called your office. During your conversation with him, he informed you that one of the girls on Maryville's soccer team, Candy Vice, had just passed out on the soccer field before the game was scheduled to begin.

You immediately left your office and drove to Morningside High to see what you could do to help Candy and the rest of the team. When you arrived at the soccer field, Candy's coach approached you and informed you that Candy was just fine. He commented that she had probably fainted because she had taken one of her mother's Valium pills just before the soccer game.

He mentioned to you that he had been informed by Candy's father that Candy often relied on her mother's Valium to calm her down, especially prior to an important game. The father told the coach that he did not think it was a problem for Candy to take the Valium as long as it did not interfere with her performance on the field.

You were uncomfortable with the fact that Candy had taken Valium before the game and you recommended to the soccer coach that Candy sit out the game. In fact, you suggested that he contact Candy's parents so that they could pick her up from Morningside and take her home.

The coach told you to mind your own business and stay out of his affairs. He stated that in his opinion Candy was just fine and that he intended for her to play the entire game.

You left the soccer field and returned to your high school to report the incident to the principal. When you arrived at Maryville High, you were met by the principal and two school board members. They mentioned to you that they had heard about the incident at the soccer field and that they had already spoken with the principal of Morningside High. They considered the matter closed and told you that if you valued your job as assistant principal, you should follow their advice by simply forgetting the whole matter and not mentioning the incident to anyone.

QUESTIONS TO CONSIDER

1. What are some of your specific concerns regarding this case?
2. Will you contact the superintendent of the school district and inform him of the incident?
3. What will you do if some of the parents of the girls' soccer team hear about the incident?

4. Why do you think the school board members were at the high school with the principal when you returned to the school?
5. Will you contact the principal at Morningside again? If so, what will you tell him?
6. Will you discipline Candy for possessing Valium at a school function?

7. Do you believe the girls' soccer coach handled the situation correctly? Why or why not?
8. What are the legal implications in this case?
9. What are the moral and ethical implications in this case?
10. Will you follow the advice of the principal and school board members and ignore the incident? Why or why not?

Suggested Activity

Conduct an inventory of your personal and professional qualities and determine how they would influence your role as an educational administrator.

Case Analysis Framework

1. Summarize the case.
2. Identify the problem in a single sentence.
3. Select specific information from the case and categorize it according to people, place, or program.
4. Review and prioritize the information.
5. Refer to the data in each category to solve the problem identified in the case and to respond to the case study questions.

Notes

Case 30

There's a New Gal in Town

The Mariner View School District is a large urban school district with an enrollment of 125,000 students. Since the late 1970s, the district has been operating under a court-mandated desegregation program that, for the most part, has relied on busing to achieve its objective. Non-Anglo students have been bused to mostly Anglo schools; however, very few Anglo students have been transported to non-Anglo schools in spite of the fact that magnet schools have been created to attract these students.

Recently, the court-ordered mandate for integrating the school district has been lifted and the district is in the process of devising a strategy to respond to the change. Since 1977, the demographics of the school district have changed from a population of 34 percent non-Anglo to the present figure of 70 percent.

When the native language of the students is taken into account, the same pattern occurs. Twelve percent of the student population was identified as Limited English Proficient in 1977. Today 35 percent of the students are identified as Limited English Proficient. There has also been a significant increase in the number of children who receive financial assistance from the government over the past 20 years.

One of the elementary schools in the district, Pacific Cove, reflects the same demographic transformation as the general community. The school has an enrollment of 475 students, of whom 68 percent are non-Anglo. Thirty-seven percent of the student body are limited in their English language skills and represent various spoken languages other than English. At least one-third of the student population is bused to Pacific Cove under the desegregation program.

Assume for this case that you are the principal of Pacific Cove Elementary School.

THE PROBLEM

For the most part, the faculty and staff have functioned in a status-quo mode for the past 15 years, and they are not motivated to change the way they operate. This includes teaching, interacting with parents, and following recommendations from school administrators. Very few of the teachers have achieved graduate school status; they have been satisfied to be left alone by district office personnel. The school has a reputation for low visibility, a complacent relationship with the community, and student test scores that fall below the mean for the district.

You have just been hired by the school district as the school site principal for Pacific Cove Elementary School. You moved your family to the area recently and you are looking forward to your new assignment. You are informed by the superintendent that you are the first minority to be hired as an administrator in the school district and that you should feel quite fortunate to have been selected among so many distinguished applicants for the position.

You have been instructed by the superintendent to bring life to a lifeless school, create a community relations program, and work diligently to raise student test scores.

You learn early on that the history of the school includes brief tenures for the previous administrators. You replaced a principal who had been at the school for only one year, and the principal before him had been at Pacific Cove for only two years. This apparently had been the pattern for a number of years.

When you first arrived at the school, the teachers greeted you with skepticism, the staff with suspicion, and the students with curiosity. After all, they had seen principals come and go and you were just another new gal in town.

The parents in the community assumed a wait-and-see attitude, and they were particularly interested in whether or not you could relate to the non-Anglo students in the school.

QUESTIONS TO CONSIDER

1. What is the primary leadership challenge in this case?
2. Describe how you would build trust with the staff.
3. What style of leadership should you use when working with the community?
4. How would you respond to the superintendent who informed you of your hiring status?
5. What would you do to bring the various groups at your school together to form one cohesive team?
6. What steps would you take to improve student achievement?
7. Identify what you believe are the reasons for the brief tenure of the principals at Pacific Cove?
8. How will you work with your school and the community to responding to the recent decision to discontinue the desegregation program?
9. What will you do to bring life to the school?
10. How will you bring the various ethnic groups together at Pacific Cove?

Suggested Activity

Develop an agenda for a meeting with representatives from the community, faculty, staff, and parents from Pacific Cove. The purpose of the meeting is to build community support and ethnic harmony.

Case Analysis Framework

1. Summarize the case.
2. Identify the problem in a single sentence.
3. Select specific information from the case and categorize it according to people, place, or program.
4. Review and prioritize the information.
5. Refer to the data in each category to solve the problem identified in the case and to respond to the case study questions.

Notes

Case 31

Before You Go, There Is One More Thing You Need to Know

The Rainbow School District is unlike most of the school districts in the area. The employees have remained dedicated to the schools for a very long time, and there is an exceptionally amicable relationship between the administration and teachers. The principal of the only high school in the district, Dickinson High School, has provided leadership based on two principles. The first is to provide quality educational programs for the students, and the second is to continue to offer emotional support to the people who work at the high school.

It is not uncommon to find the district office personnel, school site administrators, and teachers from the Rainbow School District enjoying membership in the same organizations that raise money for charitable causes and donate time to worthy events. Just recently, the Optimist Club worked diligently to produce a play. Many of the district's employees appeared in the theatrical production that drew a huge crowd and raised $20,000 for the local children's hospital burn ward.

Rainbow is the kind of school district that does not receive a great deal of media attention, maintains a steady reputation for its athletic performance, and boasts of its ethnic diversity. The superintendent and his wife are often seen at community events, and they have recently been nominated as the community's most charitable couple.

Assume for this case that you are the principal of Dickinson High School.

THE PROBLEM

Among Rainbow's most noted accomplishments is its commitment to the arts, including the production of plays presented by the high school's drama department. Mrs. Emily Katherine, the department chair, along with a dedicated group of parents have produced plays featuring the best of the playwrights.

The community is supportive of Emily's work, and several of her students have pursued careers in acting and starred in Broadway productions. Most recently, one of her graduates was featured in a local production of *Les Misérables*. Additionally, Emily offers coaching and emotional support to the district personnel who participate in the Optimist Club's play, and she virtually walks the actors through each of their respective parts.

Although Emily is known for working long hours and demanding excellence of her students, she has recently allowed her students to leave rehearsal early and arrive later than usual. One of the parent volunteers has noticed that Emily has not been herself lately and that she seems to be tired and not as alert as she used to be. When the parent confronted Emily and asked if she was feeling well, Emily responded by shrugging her shoulders and informing the parent that she was more tired than usual and that she had just recovered from the flu.

About the same time, the superintendent's wife attended a charity luncheon sponsored by the high school's drama department, and she overheard two of the teachers from the high school discussing Emily's health. According to the teachers, Emily recently had been diagnosed with multiple sclerosis and she was trying to keep it a secret.

On returning home from the luncheon, the superintendent's wife mentioned the conversation she overheard to her husband. He immediately contacted Emily's husband, who was also a teacher in the district, and asked if what his wife had heard about Emily was true. The husband confirmed the report but did not want the superintendent to mention their discussion to Emily. He reminded the superintendent that Emily had given her best years to the school and to her students because this was what she loved. He believed that she would be devastated if the news about her health was revealed to the students or the parents at the school. Emily had told her husband that she wanted to teach for as long as she could and that she was determined to pursue the life that she loved.

The superintendent directed his administrative assistant to contact you and request that you report to his office after school the same day. When you arrived at the superintendent's office, he informed you of Emily's illness.

He instructed you not to mention this matter to any of the teachers, students, or parents who were associated with the high school. He also mentioned that Emily would have a position in the school district for as long as she wanted to work. He informed you to provide a substitute teacher for Emily whenever she needed one and to be certain to offer her additional support.

After receiving the news, you stood up and began to leave the superintendent's office when the superintendent said, "Before you go, there is one more thing you need to know." He added the following statement, "It isn't often that someone like Emily Katherine comes along. She lights up a classroom and fills her students' minds with wonder." He added, "My son Brian was enrolled in Emily's class four years ago. I believe the gift she gave to my son will remain with him for all of his life. Emily Katherine is meant to teach and teach she will. Anything less would be a denial to other children of the same remarkable experience that she gave to my son. Because of Emily, Brian loves to learn. She helped him find that desire and for that I will always be grateful."

QUESTIONS TO CONSIDER

1. What steps would you take to provide support for Emily without drawing attention to her illness?
2. Would you place Emily on an alternative assignment if she requested it?
3. What role would you take in working with the teachers at the high school to honor her request for privacy regarding her illness?
4. What do you foresee as Emily's greatest challenge?
5. What is your obligation to Emily and to her students?
6. As the principal, how can you offer additional support to Emily?
7. At what point do you speak with Emily's husband?
8. How would you respond if a teacher at the high school mentioned to you that he knew about Emily's illness?
9. What would you do if a parent approached you on the same subject?
10. How would you correspond with the superintendent regarding the special circumstances surrounding Emily's illness?

Suggested Activity

Research your district's policy on health-related issues involving confidentiality for staff.

Case Analysis Framework

1. Summarize the case.
2. Identify the problem in a single sentence.
3. Select specific information from the case and categorize it according to people, place, or program.
4. Review and prioritize the information.
5. Refer to the data in each category to solve the problem identified in the case and to respond to the case study questions.

Notes

Case 32

Voucher as the Voice of the People

The inner-city housing project in Templeton has been condemned, and the city council is considering a proposal to build a new, low-income housing development. Local gangs have staked out their territory, and it is very clear to everyone in Templeton who rules what corner and for how long. The line drawn between racial boundaries is distinct and well defined by the teens that rival with their peers to dominate Templeton's turf.

Because the state approved a voucher program that would award funds to low-income families so they could choose to send their children to private schools, the school board has decided to list this subject as one of the discussion items at the next school board meeting.

The superintendent and the school board are not concerned about students leaving 54th Street High School. Even though it is the only public high school in Templeton, there have been only a handful of parents who are disgruntled. Additionally, the district is convinced that the parents will not use vouchers to send their children to the only other high school in the area, which is a private Catholic high school, St. John's.

Assume for this case that you work at the district office and have been appointed by the superintendent to meet with a group of dissatisfied parents.

THE PROBLEM

Harry Bee is a graduate of 54th Street High School and a businessman in the area who launched an aggressive campaign to support the state's voucher system. He has personally accepted credit for the passage of the ballot initiative. He boasts on a regular basis that the only thing he ever received from his experience at 54th Street High School was the opportunity to skip afternoon classes so he could hang out with his buddies and drink beer. Fortunately, Harry turned his life around, and, after graduating from high school, he developed a software program that legalized E-commerce gambling. The rest is history.

After the voters approved the voucher system in his district and, subsequently in the state, Harry left Templeton with his childhood sweetheart Vickie Lou and moved to Chicago.

During the past five years, while big-mouth Harry Bee was bragging about his accomplishments, Wilma Max and her friends were developing a list of concerns to take to the local school board that addressed what they believed were critical problems at the high school. They informed the school board that they wanted safer schools, improved academic programs, and better leadership.

Mr. Bruno, the principal of 54th Street High School, informed the school board that, in spite of Wilma's concerns, he believed that the parents of the 54th Street High

School students were too busy finding jobs, feeding themselves, and keeping track of their children to pay attention to how the district does its job.

The school board agreed with Mr. Bruno and ignored the complaints. They dismissed Wilma's concerns and those of her friends, considering them nosy zealots who had nothing better to do than to stick their noses in the business of people who knew what they were doing.

After Wilma left the first school board meeting, she formed a group called "In My Backyard" (IMBY). The group grew from 10 to 75 members, and within 3 years the IMBYs were meeting on a regular basis on behalf of their neighborhood and their schools.

Meanwhile, Mr. Bruno agreed to meet with Wilma's group on a semiregular basis, but nothing ever came of the meetings except Mr. Bruno's comment, "Thank you, ladies, for coming. See you soon."

The IMBYs decided that they had had enough of the school board, the superintendent, and the 54th Street High School principal. They began a campaign to promote St. John's High School and encouraged parents in the neighborhood to use their vouchers to pay tuition to St. John's.

When the next school year began, the enrollment at 54th Street High School dropped by 250 students, and the enrollment at St John's increased by about the same amount.

You have been instructed by the superintendent to meet with the IMBYs.

QUESTIONS TO CONSIDER

1. Do you need to develop a relationship with Wilma and her friends?
2. What information do you take back to the superintendent and the board?
3. How will you gather data from the IMBs that will prove beneficial in developing a plan to keep the parents from sending their children to St. John's?
4. What other individuals will you speak to regarding your assignment?
5. How will you advise the school board on this matter?
6. What impact could the voucher program have on the school district?
7. What can you do to put an end to the declining enrollment?
8. Will you develop a relationship with the administrators at St. John's? Why or why not?
9. What do you plan to do if the voucher system develops further to include additional families in the area?
10. Do you believe that Mr. Bruno handled the concerns of the community appropriately? Why or why not?

Suggested Activities

1. Develop a strategic plan to address the issue of the voucher program and its impact.
2. Develop a plan for your school that focuses on marketing your school to parents who have a choice between public and private school placement.

Case Analysis Framework

1. Summarize the case.
2. Identify the problem in a single sentence.
3. Select specific information from the case and categorize it according to people, place, or program.
4. Review and prioritize the information.
5. Refer to the data in each category to solve the problem identified in the case and to respond to the case study questions.

Notes

Case 33

To Brian, in His Memory

Riverdale is located beyond the city and just below the mountain range that surrounds the valley of Buena Vista. It is not uncommon to see children on their way home from school riding horses or piling into the back of a truck seemingly enjoying the innocence of youth.

The population consists of some long-time residents and a few newcomers who have moved to Riverdale to escape the city. The community shares one high school, one middle school, and three elementary schools.

The Friday night football games are attended by almost everyone in town, and at these events supportive booster club members sell raffle tickets or ask for donations for needy families in the immediate area. Most of the parents are employed in modest jobs and enjoy spending their weekends with their children.

One of the highlights of the fall season is the traditional spaghetti dinner held at the middle school, which draws a large crowd and raises money to purchase uniforms for the state and nationally recognized high school band.

Riverdale is a quiet place, secluded from the rest of the world. The people who are lucky enough to live in this community are grateful for what they have; they do not really expect much from the outside.

Assume for this case that you are the principal of the high school.

THE PROBLEM

After the football games on Friday nights, the varsity football players frequently piled into the backs of their pickup trucks and headed for the riverbed. They have been doing this for years, and no one seemed to pay much attention to the ritual. After all, the fathers of the football players did it too, and their fathers before them.

After one of the biggest games of the season, and after scoring the winning touchdown, Brian grabbed a beer from his dad's refrigerator and jumped into his truck. It was his turn to pick up his buddies and drive them to the riverbed.

This time, however, he did not reach his destination. Instead, Brian drove much too fast and missed a curve he had successfully negotiated a hundred times before. Brian's truck flipped over and he was thrown from the vehicle.

Brian's neighbor, Sue Canner, on her way home from the game, noticed Brian's truck on the side of the road. She immediately turned her car around and drove back to the high school for help. She spotted the football coach, Mr. Bailey, who was getting into his car. She told him what she had seen, and they called 911. Within 10 minutes the local paramedics arrived at the scene of the accident. They found Brian still clutching the beer in his hand. He had already stopped breathing.

Mr. Bailey contacted Brian's parents and informed them of the tragedy. The irony of this incident was that Brian's father had just sponsored a luncheon for the parents of the football players, and the keynote speaker was a representative from the group Mothers Against Drunk Driving.

Three days later you dismissed school two hours early because you had scheduled an afternoon memorial service to be held in the gymnasium for Brian. Later that evening, and in honor of Brian, the football players drove to the riverbed. With beer in hand, each player repeated these words, "To Brian, in his memory."

QUESTIONS TO CONSIDER

1. What is the responsibility of the school site administrator for educating students about drinking and driving?
2. What is the responsibility of parents for educating their children about drinking and driving?
3. What could the students have done to take responsibility for their own actions?
4. Do you believe the ritual that Brian and his friends practice is common in America's high schools?
5. What can you do as a school administrator to work with teachers to increase awareness of the dangers of drinking and driving?
6. What do you believe is the most important lesson for Brian's friends? Did they learn their lesson?
7. Do you believe that Brian's friends will continue to drink and drive?
8. Do you hold Brian's parents responsible for Brian's accident?
9. What is the role of a coach in addressing the issue of drinking and driving?
10. Do you believe it was appropriate for the principal to schedule a memorial service in the high school gymnasium during school hours?

Suggested Activity

Present this case to parents of high school students and develop a plan to prevent a similar tragedy.

Case Analysis Framework

1. Summarize the case.
2. Identify the problem in a single sentence.
3. Select specific information from the case and categorize it according to people, place, or program.
4. Review and prioritize the information.
5. Refer to the data in each category to solve the problem identified in the case and to respond to the case study questions.

Notes

Case 34

Mrs. Bumble and Her Band of Busybodies

St. Petersburg has relied on federal funds to subsidize the majority of its programs for students who qualify for federal assistance. One initiative that has been introduced to the largest school district in the city is the computer lab, which provides 60 computer stations and one instructor. Other programs include the free and reduced-cost lunch and breakfast programs provided to students each school day.

The community is proud of its students and has successfully applied for and received grants from the National Science Foundation (NSF), the Montgomery League, and the local chapter of the Woman's Democratic Caucus.

In close proximity to St. Petersburg is the small but rather influential community of Dunsberry, which happens to have as one of its distinguished residents the governor of the state. The majority of Dunsberry's citizens have lobbied for years to convince the governor to take the message of local control of federal funds to the federal level.

Recently, the federal government recommended and approved a program that allows individual states to decide on how to use some of the federal funds. The initiative lifted the federal restrictions attached to federal funding and allowed states more leniency in how federal funds are spent to provide educational programs and services to students enrolled in public schools.

The Dunsberry Unified School District was pleased to hear of this initiative, whereas the St. Petersburg community feared the consequences of the federal government's decision.

Assume for this case that you are the principal in Dunsberry.

THE PROBLEM

For many years Dunsberry and St. Petersburg have remained distant cousins. The conservative environment of Dunsberry and the liberal atmosphere of St. Petersburg have divided the communities and the school districts.

When the citizens of Dunsberry heard about the federal government's intentions to allow states to decide the best use of federal funds, they immediately formed an advisory committee. The purpose of this group was to convince the school district's elementary school principal to stop providing free and reduced-cost lunches to the students who qualified for it under the federal assistance program. The committee was chaired by Mrs. Bumble.

The members of the advisory committee were parents from the community who believed that it was not the government's responsibility to feed students but rather it was the responsibility of the parents. They were convinced that instead of using the money to feed students they could use the funds to build a computer lab just like the one that St. Petersburg had in its school district.

The first item on the Dunsberry Advisory Committee's agenda was to meet with you and lobby for their position. At the meeting, you explained to the group your understanding of the federal government's position on the subject.

You informed the advisory committee members that, although the federal government had removed some of its control over certain categories, it had no intention of turning over the free and reduced-cost lunch program to the states. You explained that the federal government was clear from the beginning that funds that would be used to provide food to students were not to be interfered with and that students who qualified for the program were to continue to receive their lunches at the federal government's expense.

You added that you would not end the program even if you could because you could see the benefit of the program for the students. You made the recommendation to Mrs. Bumble and her advisory committee that the school would be better served if the committee focused on curriculum matters and left the nourishment of students to the government.

Mrs. Bumble was not pleased with your response to the committee's inquiry, so she decided to take the matter to a higher level. The next day she contacted the governor's office and set up an appointment with him. Considering that the governor was Mrs. Bumble's neighbor and that her husband had played golf with the governor just last week, this was not a difficult meeting to arrange.

At the meeting, Mrs. Bumble shared her concern about the federal government's role in feeding students and informed the governor that she represented a very influential group of parents who shared her concern. She encouraged the governor to take the matter directly to the federal government officials. She added as she left his office that he should also speak with Dunsberry's superintendent to convince the superintendent to fire you.

QUESTIONS TO CONSIDER

1. As the elementary school principal, what is your role in deciding the distribution of federal funds at your school?
2. Do you believe you handled the meeting with the advisory committee in a constructive manner?
3. What would you have done differently?
4. Would you contact the superintendent regarding this matter?
5. What are your concerns, given the fact that Mrs. Bumble is on friendly terms with the governor?
6. What is your position regarding the state control of federal funds?
7. Do you believe that the federal government should have less jurisdiction over some of the federally funded programs? If so, which ones?
8. How would you react if the federal government stopped providing funds for free and reduced-cost lunches to students in the public school system?
9. Do you believe this program has an influence on the students' ability to achieve in school?
10. As the principal, do you believe it is appropriate to discuss political topics such as federal versus state funding of school programs with the parents of the students at your school?

Suggested Activity

Write a position paper on the use of power by special interest groups and how it influences the role of school administrators.

Case Analysis Framework

1. Summarize the case.
2. Identify the problem in a single sentence.
3. Select specific information from the case and categorize it according to people, place, or program.
4. Review and prioritize the information.
5. Refer to the data in each category to solve the problem identified in the case and to respond to the case study questions.

Notes

Suggested Readings

The following suggested readings are arranged according to the topics identified in the matrix in Figure 1 (page 3).

Curriculum and Instruction

Bagnato, S., Neisworth, S. M., & Munson, S. M. (1989). *Linking developmental assessment and early intervention: Curriculum-based prescriptions* (2nd ed.). Rockville, MD: Aspen Systems Corp.

Becker, H. J. (1990). *Opportunities for learning curriculum and instruction in middle grade schools.* Baltimore, MD: Center for Research on Elementary and Middle Schools, Johns Hopkins University.

Bryson, J. E., & Bentley, C. (1980). *Ability grouping of public school students: Legal aspects of classification and tracking methods.* Charlottesville, VA: Michie.

Glatthorn, A. A. (1997). *The principal as curriculum leader: Shaping what is taught or tested.* Thousand Oaks, CA: Corwill.

Henderson, J. G., & Hawthorne, R. D. (1995). *Transformative curriculum leadership.* Englewood, NJ: Merrill.

Leadership

Ackerman, R. H., Donaldson, G. A. Jr., & Van Der Bogert, R. (1996). *Making sense as a school leader: Persisting questions, creative opportunities.* San Francisco, CA: Jossey-Bass.

Ashbaugh, C., & Kasten, K. L. (1995). *Educational leadership: Case studies for reflective practice* (2nd ed). White Plains, NY: Longman.

Blase, J. R. (1998). *Handbook of instructional leadership: How really good principals promote teaching and learning.* Thousand Oaks, CA: Corwin.

Cohen, F. L. (1987). *From the classroom to the principal's office: Growing pains.* Springfield, IL: Thomas.

Mulkeen, T. A., Cambron-McCabe, N. H., & Anderson, B. J. (1994). *Democratic leadership: The changing context of administrative preparation.* Norwood, NJ: Ablex.

Employee Relations

Blase, J., & Blase, J. R. (1994). *Empowering teachers: What successful principals do.* Thousand Oaks, CA: Corwin.

Doherty, R. E. (Ed.). (1967). *Employer-employee relations in the public schools.* Ithaca, NY: Cornell.

Finchum, R. N. (1961). *School plant manager: Administering the custodial program.* Washington, DC: U.S. Department of Health, Education and Welfare, Office of Education.

Kestner, P. B. (Ed.). (1988). *Education and mediation: Exploring the alternatives.* Washington, DC: American Bar Association.

Peairs, R. (Ed.). (1974). *Avoiding conflict in faculty personnel practices.* San Francisco, CA: Jossey-Bass.

Race and Gender Relations

Abraham, J. (1995). *Divide and school.* Washington DC: Palmer.

Horgan, D. D. (1995). *Achieving gender equity: Strategies for the classroom.* Boston, MA: Allyn and Bacon.

Matzen, S. P. (1965). *The relationship between racial composition and scholastic achievement in elementary school classrooms.* Ann Arbor, MI: University Microfilms.

Purvis, J., & Hales, M. (Eds.). (1983). *The achievement and inequality in education: A reader.* London: Routledge & Kegan Paul.

Romo, H. (1997). *Improving ethnic and racial relations in the schools.* Charleston, WV: ERIC Clearinghouse on Rural and Small Schools.

Student Conduct

Artz, S. (1999). *Sex, power, and the violent school girl.* New York: Teachers College.

Besag, V. E. (1988). *Bullies and victims in schools: A guide to understanding and management.* Philadelphia, PA: Open University.

Bodine, R. (1998). *The handbook of conflict resolution education: A guide to building quality programs in schools.* San Francisco, CA: Jossey-Bass.

Bybee, R. W. (1982). *Violence, values, and justice in the schools.* Boston, MA: Allyn and Bacon.

Health and Welfare

Breckon, D. J., Harvey, J. R., & Lancaster, R. B. (1985). *Community health education: Settings, roles, and skills.* Rockville, MD: Aspen Systems Corp.

Howard, G. S., & Nathan, P. E. (Eds.). (1994). *The alcohol use and misuse by young adults.* Notre Dame, IN: University of Notre Dame.

Rafool, M. (1999). *Funding coordinated school health programs.* Denver, CO: National Conference of State Legislatures.

U.S. Congress House Committee on Education Labor. (1984). *Extending and improving the national School Lunch Act and Child Nutrition Act of 1966.* Washington, DC: U.S. Government Printing Office.

Community Relations

Bennett, L. M. (1977). *Keeping in touch with parents: Teachers' best friend.* Austin, TX: Learning Concepts.

Celebuski, C., Farn, E., & Burns, S. (1998). *Status of education reform in public elementary and secondary schools: Principals' perspectives.* Washington, DC: U.S. Department of Education Research and Improvement.

Pawlas, G. (1995). *The administrator's guide to school-community relations.* Princeton, NJ: Eye on Education.

Rutherford, W. L. (1983). *In search of understanding their role*. Austin, TX: Research and Development Center for Teacher Education.

Wolfe, L. G. (1982). *Communicating with the community: Keys to school boardsmanship, a program of continuing education for school board members*. Portland, OR: Northwest Regional Educational Laboratory.

Budget and Finance

Alexand, K., & Jordan, K. F. (1973). *Constitutional reform of school finance*. Lexington, MA: Lexington.

Augenblick, J., Gold, S. D., & McGuire, K. (1990). *Education finance in the 1990s*. Denver, CO: Education Commission of the States.

Bliss, S. W. (1978). *Zero-base budgeting: A management tool for school districts*. Chicago, IL: Research Corporation of the Association of School Business Officials.

David, M. E. (1975). *School rule: A case study of participation in budgeting in America*. Cambridge, MA: Ballinger.

Mosborg, S. (1996). *How money matters to school performance*. Portland, OR: Northwest Regional Educational Laboratory.

Conflict Management

Girard, K. L., & Koch, S. J. (1996). *Conflict resolution in the schools: A manual for educators*. San Francisco, CA: Jossey-Bass.

Lawrence, C. E., & Vachon, M. K. (1995). *How to handle staff misconduct: A step-by-step guide*. Thousand Oaks, CA: Corwin.

Romo, H. (1997). *Dealing sensitively with ethnic conflicts: Mexican American and African American tensions*. Charleston, WV: ERIC Clearinghouse on Rural Education and Small Schools.

Schriro, D. B. (1985). *Safe schools, sound schools: Learning in a non-disruptive environment*. New York: ERIC Clearinghouse on Urban Education.

Wolf, E. P. (Ed.). (1976). *Conflicts and tensions in the public schools*. Beverly Hills, CA: Sage.

Ethics

Deal, T. E., & Peterson, K. D. (1999). *Shaping school culture: The heart of leadership*. San Francisco, CA: Jossey- Bass.

Kimbrough, R. B. (1985). *Ethics: A course of study for educational leaders*. Arlington, VA: American Association of School Administrators.

McCall, J. R. (1986). *The provident principal*. Chapel Hill, NC: Institute of Government, University of North Carolina.

Strike, K. A., Haller, E. J., & Soltis, J. F. (1998). *The ethics of school administration* (2nd ed.). New York: Teachers College.

Governance and Politics

Adams, N. (1984). *Law and teachers today* (2nd ed.). London: Hutchinson.

Duttweiler, P. C. (1988). *The dysfunctions of bureaucratic structure*. Washington, DC: U.S. Department Office of Educational Research and Improvement, Educational Resources Information Center.

Harmer, D. (1994). *School choice: Why you need it—How you get it*. Washington, DC: Cato Institute.

Imber, M., & Van Gell, T. (1993). *Education law*. New York: McGraw-Hill.

Special Education

Barnes, D. B., & Barnes C. K. (1990). *Special educator's survival guide: Practical techniques and material for supervision and instruction*. West Nyack, NY: Center for Applied Research in Education.

Bootel, J. A. (1995). *CEC special advocacy handbook*. Reston, VA: Council for Exceptional Children.

Chalfant, J. C., & Van Dusen Pysh, M. (1980). *The compliance manual: A guide to the rules and regulations of the Education for All Handicapped Act, Public Law 94-142: Questions, answers, and recommended practices*. New Rochelle, NY: Pem.

Diversity

Baéz, T., Fernandez, R. R., & Guskin, J. T. (1986). *Desegregation and Hispanic students*. Rossalyn, VA: National Clearinghouse for Bilingual Education.

Grugeon, E., & Woods, P. *Multicultural perspective in the primary school*. New York: Routledge.

Lee, C. D. (1994). *Multicultural education challenges to administrators and school leaders: Urban education program*. Oak Brook, IL.: North Central Regional Educational Laboratory. Washington, DC: U.S. Department of Education, Office of Educational Research and Improvement, Educational Resources Information Center.

McGlashan, P. (1998). *Biodiversity counts: Teacher's guide*. New York: The Museum.

Ngcongo, R. G. P. (1995). *Educational leadership for schools: An African perspective*. Pietermaritzburg, South Africa: Reach Out Publishers.

Technology

Bates, T. (1995). *Technology, open learning, and distance education*. New York: Routledge.

Griliches, Z. (1995). *Technology, education, and productivity*. San Francisco, CA: ICS Press.

Kent, T. W., & McNergney R. F. (1999). *Will technology really change education?* Thousand Oaks, CA: Corwin.

Thompson, S. D. (Ed.). (1995). *Principals for our changing schools: The knowledge and skills base*. Fairfax, VA: National Policy Board for Educational Administration.

Index